FAITHFULNESS

34 Faith Principles From Hebrews 11 to Help You On Your Pilgrimage to Glory

Dr. Jon Kile

Wise Media Group
Morro Bay, California

FAITHFULNESS: *34 Faith Principles From Hebrews 11 to Help You On Your Pilgrimage to Glory*

© Copyright 2022 Jon Kile

ISBN: 978-1629672502 (Paperback)
ISBN: 978-1629672533 (Hardcover)
Library of Congress Control Number: 2022912876

Scripture taken from the New King James Version®. Copyright © 1982 by Thomas Nelson. Used by permission. All rights reserved.

All rights reserved. No part of this book may be reproduced in any form or by any electronic or mechanical means, including information storage and retrieval systems, without written permission from the author, except in the case of a reviewer, who may quote brief passages embodied in critical articles or in a review.

Trademarked names may appear throughout this book. Rather than use a trademark symbol with every occurrence of a trademarked name, names are used in an editorial fashion, with no intention of infringement of the respective owner's trademark.

The information in this book is distributed on an "as is" basis, without warranty. Although every precaution has been taken in the preparation of this work, neither the author nor the publisher shall have any liability to any person or entity with respect to any loss or damage caused or alleged to be caused directly or indirectly by the information contained in this book.

Edited by Troy Swauger
Cover design by Tatiana Fernandez
Produced for Wise Media Group by Brian Schwartz

v8.12

To my wife, Tiffany, my ideal travelling partner throughout this fast and fading life. She loves her Lord with passion and fervor, and she is a great inspiration to me as I seek to faithfully glorify and honor my King. I am truly blessed.

TABLE OF CONTENTS

Introduction vii
Chapter 1 1
Chapter 2 9
Chapter 3 17
Chapter 4 31
Chapter 5 47
Chapter 6 57
Chapter 7 71
Chapter 8 79
Chapter 9 99
Chapter 10 119
Chapter 11 137
Chapter 12 147
Chapter 13 155
Chapter 14 167
Chapter 15 183
Chapter 16 207
Conclusion 219
APPENDIX: Faith Principles from Hebrews 11 225
Bibliography 229

INTRODUCTION

The goal of this book is to encourage you in your Christian faith. Life is fleeting and we only get one opportunity here to live out our faith in God. In glory we will walk by sight (can't wait), but until then, we walk by faith. Let's walk well. Do we really want to get to the end of our lives and find that we wasted most of it on earthly things; things that fade away and mean nothing in eternity? We certainly don't want to get to the end of our lives only to come to the sad realization that we lived most of our Christian faith in mediocrity and compromise. This book is meant to awaken and encourage us to radical, Biblical faithfulness. God is worthy and soon we will be in glory.

  The book of Hebrews seeks to show us that life is all about the absolute superiority of Christ in all things. Some of the original readers of Hebrews forgot this, and the book of Hebrews was their reminder, and ours. The original readers of this epistle were beginning to face some serious persecution for their faith in Christ, and the pressure to compromise, revert, give in and to go back to their old ways of empty ritualistic Judaism weighed heavy upon them. Therefore, the writer reminds them of Christ's superiority, and then he shows the readers that

Christ alone is worth living for, suffering for and even dying for. Hebrews 11 shows us what the true life of faith looks like.

The assumption in Hebrews 11 is that you have already placed your saving faith in Christ and that you are already saved. The end of chapter ten makes that clear. Verses 38-39 state:

> 'Now the just shall live by faith; But if anyone draws back, My soul has no pleasure in him.' But we are not of those who draw back to perdition, but of those who believe to the saving of the soul. (NKJV)

So what the writer says next in chapter 11 is for those who have believed to the saving of the soul. So here's the question: have you believed to the saving of the soul? Are you truly saved? Without true belief, your soul is lost and doomed to eternal wrath. We are all sinners, and sin has drastic wages, death—and not just physical death but also eternal punishment. Sin not only separates us from God, but sin condemns every person to hell, the just punishment for sin. You say, "How's that just? Hell for just one sin?" It's right and just because our God is an infinite God, and sin against an infinite God demands infinite wages. Therefore, either we pay the wages of our sin for an infinite amount of time in hell, or an infinite and truly worthy One pays for our sin once for all, which is exactly what Jesus, God the Son, did on the cross for all who believe. Indeed, 2 Corinthians 5:21 says, "For He made Him who knew no sin to be sin for us, that we might become the righteousness of God in Him." This tells us that on the cross, God treated Jesus as if He had committed every sin ever committed by every true believer, even though He committed none. This means that on the cross, the believer's sin was not only put onto Christ, but He was also punished as the believer's substitute for all that sick and vile sin.

Picture a courtroom scene. You have been accused of a crime and you are clearly guilty. It's obvious, certain and justified; for all the evidence is against you. God is the judge and Satan is the accuser. The accuser has you right where he wants you. The punishment for your crime is death, and again, the case against you is iron clad; you are guilty. The just verdict: guilty. The sentence is death, and now they are going to take you away to be executed. That's when a voice from the back rings out, "Me for him! I'll go instead. I'll take the punishment. I'll pay the penalty." Someone responds, "But You Lord did nothing wrong ever, and this person is guilty. We have him on multiple counts!" Jesus responds, "No, put it all on me, I will pay the price, I will pay the sentence of death that is required." And that's what He did on the cross for all who believe. He took our place as believers and died so we don't have to face eternity in hell. He was executed so we who believe could live forever in eternal glory. This is indeed the great exchange: our sin as believers was credited to Christ's spiritual account, which He paid for in full on the cross when He died, and His perfect righteousness was credited to our spiritual account which fits us perfectly for heaven. As believers, we gave Him our sin, and He gave us His righteousness. That's why sinners can go to heaven, even though none of us deserves to. Jesus took care of it for us as believers.

This is true good news. I cannot make myself right with God, but God can make me right through the death of Christ in my place. This amazing reality comes by faith. Faith means to believe to the extent of complete trust and reliance.[1] Biblical faith isn't just intellectual assent, but it is believing on Jesus as revealed in the Scriptures: in His person and work. Biblical saving faith is trust in Jesus Christ as a living person for forgiveness of sins and for eternal life with God. It is a personal trust in Jesus alone to

---

[1] J. P. Louw & E.A Nida, *Greek-English lexicon of the New Testament: based on semantic domains, Vol. 1,* (New York: United Bible Societies, 1988), 377.

save me from my sin that condemns me. Saving faith always includes repentance that turns away from the past sinful way of living, and then follows faithfully after the Lord. We all sin, but repentance expresses a sorrow for sin, a battle against sin and a heart that seeks to honor the Lord in the midst of battling the sin. Saving faith affects your life, and while a person is saved by faith alone, true saving faith will result in a lifestyle of loving obedience to the Lord who saved you.

I love the story of the old man who had, many years ago, been saved and delivered by the Lord. One day a young man came up and asked him what Jesus had done for him. The old man then went over to a dry pile of leaves, found a worm, and put that worm in the middle of the pile. He then lit the outside of the pile of leaves on fire. Soon the flames came closer and closer to the worm, and just before the flames reached the worm, the man plunged his hands into the pile and snatched up the worm, rescuing him from the flames. The old man then said, "I am that worm."[2] That's not only a great picture of what Jesus did for the old man, but it's also a great picture of what Jesus has done for every one of us in Christ: He rescued us, delivered us, saved us from the fire of hell and eternal wrath, and He redeemed us. How can we be indifferent or mediocre to a God who died to save us? As the saved, fervent love for Him must now compel us to live out our faith with passion until He takes us to glory. The faithful keep this in view, and they resist becoming sidetracked by the many snares of this fading life. In light of what Christ has so graciously done for undeserving sinners like us, our call is to now live faithfully for His glory until He calls us home. How could we not?

---

[2] Margaret T Applegarth, *Junior Missionary Stories*, (New York: Board of Publication and Bible School Work, 1917), p. 358.

CHAPTER 1

Puritan writer John Bunyan got it right in his Christian allegorical novel, Pilgrim's Progress, when he likened the believer's life as a long journey filled with hills and valleys, hardships and blessings. In Bunyan's classic, the pilgrimage began before the main character, Christian, had been saved, and it ended when he arrived at Celestial City, the thinly veiled reference to heaven. Not only is this imagery Biblical, but if you have ever been on a long and arduous hike, you know how true to life Bunyan's imagery presents.

I experienced this in 2016 when I hiked the John Muir Trail with my buddy, Dave. The John Muir Trail is a long-distance natural path that climbs through California's majestic Sierra Nevada. It begins in the valley of Yosemite National Park and stretches 213.7 miles before it ends at the 14,505-foot summit of Mount Whitney, the tallest mountain in the contiguous United States. The trail inflicts a total elevation gain of approximately 47,000 feet.[3] The

---

[3] Elizabeth Wenk, *John Muir Trail* (Birmingham: Wilderness press, 2014), 1.

360-degree view from the crest of Whitney is stunning, but the effort to reach it remains absolutely brutal. Hikers travel the trail in both directions, their starting point dependent upon personal preference, the time of year, the quota system and the weather forecasts. Dave and I had always planned to start at the northern terminus, in the Yosemite Valley and move south. The National Park Service indicates most hikers average three weeks to cover the distance. We wanted to finish it in 15 days. We expected it would be a struggle, we just never guessed how much.

Once we'd decided to make the hike, we began the process of collecting the necessary permits, a bureaucratic nightmare, which ultimately required a Yosemite wilderness permit, a Whitney trail permit and a California fishing license in case we got lucky.

As we waited, we began to train and plan in earnest. Dave runs nearly every day and has competed in ultramarathons; races where competitors will run as much as 100 miles. For as long as I've known him, Dave has been in excellent shape. I run and have a solid workout regimen that I follow, so I do okay, but by the time the hike was upon us, I was still heavier than I'd wanted and felt underprepared. I had no idea what I was in for. When you hike the John Muir Trail, there is no way you can carry enough food on your back to survive the whole trail. You're required to carry food in a bear-proof canister for most of the trip, which limits how much you can bring. Veteran hikers set at least two resupply points along the trail. They either send their supplies ahead to designated spots or have someone bring food to them. Our plan was to resupply ourselves only once. To do this, we'd enlisted a friend and his son, who would have to drive about four hours through the lower Sierra range, with the last portion along a one-lane road to a lake. They had to cross the lake aboard a water taxi and then hike a mile through the wilderness to meet us along the trail. Being re-supplied only once meant we had to ration our food wisely.

Breakfast consisted of two packets of instant oatmeal and coffee, while lunch involved two Clif bars. These were usually eaten throughout the day while we hiked. Snacks consisted of a limited supply of almonds and beef jerky. For dinner we shared a double-portion Mountain House instant meal. This isn't a lot of food, especially when expending the amount of energy used while hiking steep trails all day. But this is all we could cram into our bear canisters. The result was that we were in a constant state of hunger.

The day before our hike began, we were driven to Yosemite Valley, where we spent the night in a tent cabin in Curry Village. I didn't sleep, too nervous about what laid ahead. I had serious doubts that I could actually finish. Throughout our training, we heard of people who had planned to hike the whole trail only to bail out after three or four days. I didn't want to be like one of those, and I certainly didn't want to fail at what I was seeing as one of the biggest physical challenges I'd ever faced. I never found a position in that Yosemite tent that was comfortable and finally gave up when 3:30 a.m. came around. I was ready when the alarm went off. We stepped outdoors into the dark, slipped our backpacks on and began walking.

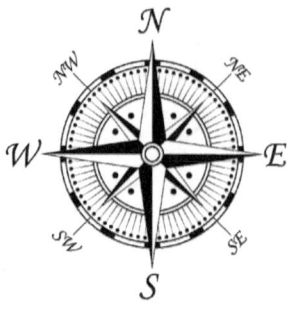

An Explanation of Biblical Faith

Hebrews 11 assumes that you are already saved by grace through faith in Christ alone because of what He did in the believer's place on the cross. It assumes that you are already walking the narrow path of the Christian faith. Once a person has believed to the saving of the soul, the rest of life is to be committed to living out that faith for the glory of God. Hebrews 11 shows us what a saved and faithful life should look like in growing measure. It is a solid blueprint of what a saved soul pursues. True faith always results in faithful living, faithful walking until glory. The opening verse of Hebrews 11 shows this truth to us by telling us, "Faith is the substance of things hoped for, the evidence of things not seen."

This tells us that true faith has substance and evidence. In this case, *substance* means to stand or to set under.[4] It describes a support, a confidence, a steadiness, an assurance and a foundation. It tells us that faith provides the firm ground on which we stand while we eagerly wait for all the amazing promises that lie ahead. In other words, true faith believes God. It relies on what God says and gives us firm ground until His promises are fully realized.

---

[4] Louw, 673.

The word *hope* means to look forward with confidence to that which is good and beneficial.[5] It means to expect with the implication of some benefit. Faith is what gives substance to our hopes. In other words, faith grabs hold of what is hoped for as something that is real and substantial. Some may ask, "Well, doesn't that definition negate what the word faith really means? I thought faith was putting your hope in something that probably won't happen. I thought faith was just a crutch for people who can't really think for themselves." Not at all! True faith is a sure confidence based on what God says. Most of my hopes as a Christian lie ahead, and those hopes are certain. Faith allows me to walk through this life triumphantly and obediently until those future hopes are realized.

The question then is, what do we hope for? We hope for the things that God has told us that we have not yet fully realized—incredible things like heaven and the glories that lie ahead. Faith looks at all of those hopes and helps us to patiently wait for them, and it gives us an assurance and confidence to patiently endure through it all until we receive those promises in full. Faith is the solid ground that allows us to confidently live for the glory of God through all the hills and valleys of this fading life.

Everyone has faith. The real issue is this: what is a worthy object of our faith? What limits do we place on our examination of truth? For Christians, our faith is in God and in what He says in His Word. We believe that God has spoken to us, and while God hasn't told us everything there is to know, He has told us enough about truth, salvation, and life, and we put our trust in Him; this God who created all, this God who knows all, this God who never lies, this God who is truth. Even though we can't see Him, we are full of confidence that what He says is real and true, and our lives reflect that reality with faithful living.

---

[5] Gerhard Kittel, *Theological Dictionary of the New Testament*, vol 2, (Grand Rapids, MI: Eerdmans Publishing, 1964), 517.

Faith is also described as the evidence of things not seen. The word *evidence* means conviction.[6] So faith is the conviction that the unseen exists. This takes things a step further for us because this implies action. True conviction is willing to stake your life on your hope. In his exposition of the Book of Hebrews, influential evangelical author A.W. Pink uses the analogy of two men standing on the deck of a ship, looking in the same direction. One sees nothing, but the other man sees a distant steamer. The difference is that the first man is looking with his unaided eye, whereas the second man is looking through a telescope. Faith is the telescope that brings the future promises of God into present focus. Faith enables us to see the unseen world that the natural man cannot see.[7] As Kent Hughes said, "True faith is a solid conviction resting on God's Words that makes the future present and the invisible seen. Faith has at its core a massive sense of certainty."[8] This is correct. For us who have put our faith in the Lord, we are confident, we are certain and we are sure for God has revealed these things to us. The Bible tells us that true faith is a gift of God (Ephesians 2:8), and those who don't have it are blinded by their sin, but those with true saving faith are certain in what God has said and done. They are so confident that they will not only live out their faith, but they will die for their faith. Such depths of faith are based on the truth of God, and it propels us forward.

When Noah entered the ark, he had the same conviction of the coming flood that he had during the 120 years it took to build the massive craft. God had spoken and that was all that mattered. He did not need to look at the clouds, he trusted God. True faith is like that. It is a conviction of things when they are not seen. Faith says, "I believe, I know, I act."

---

[6] Kittel, 474.
[7] A. W. Pink, *An Exposition of Hebrews*, (Grand Rapids, MI: Baker Book House, 1954), 652.
[8] R. Kent Hughes, *Preaching the Word: Hebrews*, (Wheaton, IL: Crossway, 2015), 288.

To show the reality of this, the writer writes these words in Hebrews 11:2, "For by it (faith), the elders obtained a good testimony." The writer's mention of the *elders* refers generally to the saints of the Old Testament, and specifically to the saints who are mentioned throughout Hebrews 11.[9] The word *testimony* means to receive praise or approval.[10] This tells us that these elders lived by faith, and therefore God approved of them. The 19th century Presbyterian minister Marvin Vincent was a theological seminary professor in New York and is best known for his word studies in the New Testament. He said, "God bore witness to them in the victory of their faith over all obstacles, and their characters and deeds as men of faith were recorded in Scripture."[11]

So God approves of those who operate on faith; of those who live out their faith in tangible ways as mentioned in Hebrews 11. I want that approval. I pray you do as well. The rest of Hebrews 11 shows us the kind of life God approves. A good testimony from God comes to those who live out their faith.

---

[9] Marvin Vincent, *Word studies in the New Testament*, vol. 4, (New York: Charles Scribner's Sons, 1887), 511.
[10] Louw, 417.
[11] Vincent, 511.

CHAPTER 2

John Muir Trail:

The John Muir Trail stretches through large swaths of alpine mountain vistas, incredible scenery that begins in Yosemite National Park, cuts through the Ansel Adams Wilderness and rises into both Kings Canyon and Sequoia national parks. Breathtaking views beckon with each mile, and everything displays the incredible glory of God's creation.

Our days started so early that the moon still floated high in the sky as a silent companion, watching over us as we stumbled behind the glow of small LED lamps that we wore as hats. We did this for a couple hours until a hint of light revealed the horizon. Each day blossomed before us, and we witnessed His wonder and creativity showcased in towering pines and thickets of aspen that would open to massive rock formations and distant waterfalls. We could see His handiwork everywhere.

On the third night, I jolted awake with light flooding the interior of my little tent. Disoriented, I fumbled around to disentangle myself from my twisted sleeping bag. I thought, "Why is Dave shining his flashlight into my tent?" But it wasn't Dave—I could hear him snoring in his tent nearby. The light was everywhere. I unzipped my tent and peered outside to discover the light that had awakened me was the moon. It was absolutely beautiful. It lit up the whole sky.

The next night we camped beside a splendid little lake. Before I went to bed, I walked over to the edge of the water and turned off my flashlight. The moonlight bounced off the surface of the lake, and my mind immediately thought of how amazing God is for creating such beauty.

On our eighth day we ran into rain. We had hiked a long day (looking back, every day was a long day) and we made camp on the shore of Evolution Lake in a place called Evolution Valley, at the base of Mount Darwin. The unrelenting rain turned to hail, driven by a frigid north wind that turned the night air colder than any other night. The bitter chill seemed to leak through the thermal lining of my sleeping bag, making sleep fitful at best.

Exhausted, we both let our usual 4:30 a.m. rising time pass and I would've ignored the outside longer, but Dave wouldn't allow it. We had another long day ahead. Did I say it was cold? The rain and hail had ceased at some point during the night, but the air remained frigid. A water bottle I'd left outside my tent flap had frozen. We struggled through our pre-dawn breaking-camp routine. The cold made everything take longer as our joints were stiff and unforgiving, and our numb fingers practically useless.

When we finally left the clearing and returned to the trail, I looked back as the sun crested over the mountain. It was incredible. The colors were red, orange, purple, yellow and everything else in between. I thought, "Of all the scenery we'd seen so far, how ironic that this place called Evolution Valley had best displayed the greatness and beauty of God's creation." I laughed aloud. Do people really think this all came about by evolution? Only a good and creative God could make something so beautiful.

Many times, during that two-week hike I would wake up in the middle of the night, crawl out of my tent and gaze upward. There in the still blackness that surrounded me the stars were remarkable. There were so many, and they seemed to connect together and form one big bright super star. I would gaze for a long time and think, "Thank you, Lord. You are amazing." Every day on the trail was a new display of God's beautiful creation. Every day I stood in awe of Him.

One of the amazing things I heard on my John Muir Trail hike was what sounded like music playing. It became a regular occurrence. I could track it playing somewhere in the distance. But I could never tell from which direction; it just seemed to be there. Sometimes I'd also hear singing. After a while I no longer questioned where it came from, just accepted the melody as a companion. Later I'd attributed this to the natural scape of the trail, which tracked alongside and crossed numerous rivers and streams. I think it was the way the water flowed over the rocks that made it sound like music. This too made me stand in awe of God. Creation really does sing forth His glory. God is so good, and His creation clearly displays that goodness.

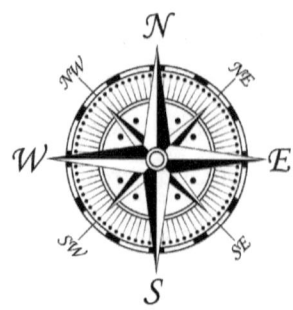

Faith Principle 1
The faithful trust in God as the Creator

God has always existed. He alone was not a created being because He has always been.[12] When God spoke to Moses from the burning bush, He described Himself in this way in Exodus 3:14, "I Am who I Am." God alone was, is, and is yet to be. Isaiah 40:28 describes Him like this: "The everlasting God, the LORD, the Creator of the ends of the earth..." He alone is the everlasting God.

When we think of a person creating something, we often think of someone who is making new things out of preexisting materials. God is different. God is the ultimate creator because He created everything that has ever existed, including the raw materials used by creators today.[13] He made the universe out of nothing. God is the one and only true Creator, and all things find their origin in God. Because of this, everything ultimately belongs to God. As humans, we are a creation of God. This truth has serious ramifications for every human being.

The writer of Hebrews said in chapter 11, verse 3, "By faith we understand that the worlds were framed by the word of God, so that the things which are seen were not made of things which are visible." Here the

---

[12] "What Does it Mean That God is the Creator?," Compelling Truth, Got Questions Ministries, accessed 7/21/2020, https://www.compellingtruth.org/Creator-God.html
[13] Ibid.

writer is telling us that the faithful put their trust in God as Creator of all things, including themselves.

This is the first of 19 uses of *by faith* in this chapter. All of the other uses of this term relate to the people of God from the Old Testament who lived out their faith in God. However, this first usage goes back to the biblical account of creation in Genesis. God did it by His Word, and that is all it took.

Genesis 1:1 says, "In the beginning God created..." These few words show us that God is central to everything. They show us that God was before everything, that everything had a beginning save God alone, that God was there before the beginning, and that God is the key subject matter of the universe.

The word *created*—as in, God created—is the Hebrew word "bara[14]," and it is always and only used for describing the work of God. "Bara", as a word, carries a unique quality that equates it to a sense of absoluteness. "Bara" to the Hebrews means that the infinite, eternal, triune God of the universe brought things into existence that had never existed before.

No one else can do that except God alone. Everything around you—your body, the trees, the flowers, the world, the stars, the moon, and everything you can see as well as everything you can't see—came into existence instantaneously out of no pre-existing material from God.

The faithful believe "the worlds were framed by the word of God." The term *worlds* is a Hebrew way of referring to the created universe, and also to periods of time as administered by God.[15] Here, the author says that faith gives us understanding of how the material universe and time came into being—namely, by God. Matter isn't eternal, God is eternal.

---

[14] T.E Mccomiskey, *Theological Wordbook of the Old Testament*, edited by R. L. Harris, G. L. Archer Jr., & B. K. Waltke, (Chicago: Moody Press: 1981), 127.
[15] Louw, 1.

And the eternal God brought physical matter and time into being by His powerful word alone. He said it and it came into being, and the faithful ones believe that. The fact that the writer puts verse 3 at the start of his list of "by faith" examples, shows us that faith in God as Creator is foundational to knowing and pleasing God. The world is not left to chance or to some impersonal fate. The world was created by an all-wise, all-powerful and loving God. Matter is not eternal but is made by a sovereign God. God is the maker, not the thing made. God is not created by man out of sticks and stones, but it is God who made man and everything else that exists in this universe. And if he made you, then you answer to Him.

Because the point appears simple, it may be glossed over, but this truth is vitally important to understand. Ever since the fall of the human race into sin, people have been in rebellion against the Creator and Lord of the universe. Pastor Steven Cole spent more than 40 years as a pastor before retiring from Arizona's Flagstaff Christian Fellowship in 2018. With his background in expository preaching and philosophy, he has trumpeted this truth throughout his ministry. He has published several articles on *AboutBible.org*. Cole notes:

> We live in a world that has brazenly cast-off God. We have cast Him off as the Creator, insisting that science proves that we all evolved from pond slime through sheer chance, billions of years ago. For if God is not the Creator, then He does not need to be obeyed. If man is the product of millions of years of chance, then he need not fear judgment or eternity ahead, because at death he

> simply ceases to exist. So if we cast aside God as the Creator, we can determine for ourselves what is right and what is wrong.[16]

He is correct. The faithful ones are those who trust God as Creator of all things, and they understand the ramifications that has on their lives.

Sadly, many today are like the family of mice who lived all their lives in a large piano.[17] The music of the instrument came to them in their piano-world, filling all the dark spaces with sound and harmony. At first the mice were impressed by it. They drew comfort and wonder from the thought that there was Someone who made the music, though invisible to them, yet close to them. They loved to think of the Great Player whom they could not see. Then one day a daring mouse climbed up part of the piano and returned very thoughtfully. He had found out how the music was made. Wires were the secret; tightly stretched wires of graduated lengths which trembled and vibrated. They must now revise all their old beliefs, and now none but the most conservative could any longer believe in the Unseen Player. No, it was the wires! Later, another explorer carried the explanation even further. Hammers were now the secret, great numbers of hammers dancing and leaping on the wires. It was hammers that made the music. This was a more complicated theory, but it all went to show that they lived in a purely mechanical and mathematical world. The Unseen Player soon came to be thought of as a myth.

Most of the people of this world are like these mice to their eternal detriment. However, not believing the truth doesn't change the truth or the ramifications for ignoring the truth. God made you and He sets the

---

[16] Steven Cole, "Upsetting the World for Christ", Acts: Lesson 43 (Acts 17:1-15), accessed on 3/13, 2020. https://bible.org/seriespage/lesson-43-upsetting-world-christ-acts-171-15.

[17] "The Mice family," Bible.org, accesses 4/14/2019. https://bible.org/illustration/mice-family.

rules as your Creator and ruler. To ignore Him is to condemn yourself to hell. The faithful are those who believe God and what He has said to us. He created everything including us, He sets the rules, and trusting in Him as Creator and ruler of our lives means that we bow down to His sovereign rule and Word. That is foundational to how we live out our faith. We believe who He is, we believe what He has told us and we understand that we will answer to Him as our Creator. Faith sees this and responds accordingly.

CHAPTER 3

John Muir Trail:

One of the main reasons for me hiking the John Muir Trail was to commune with the Lord. Life is busy, distractions abound, and it's easy to become spiritually complacent. This is always a danger for me, and that's why I need to get away on a hike. Hiking is a way for me to get refocused. Most days on the trail I found myself alone. All day. My friend Dave and I always started off together, but he's a much faster hiker than I am, and we had a routine that worked for us. Once the sun crested the horizon, he would pick up his pace and soon I would be on the trail on my own. Interestingly, I never became bored because I wasn't really alone. I prayed continually, except for the times I was so tired I couldn't think straight, which happened regularly. I sang often, praising and thanking God. One day when Dave and I met for lunch, after he'd waited an hour for me to reach his location, he said, "Jon, are you okay? I thought I heard you singing." Yep, I was fine, and yes, I was singing.

Many times, I wasn't really singing or praying as much as just meditating on God's greatness and beauty, since it was displayed right there in front of me continually. I repented often as well. I don't hate sin like I ought to hate sin, I don't battle like a warrior should battle, I fall short often, and I waste too much time. So, I regularly repented, and I renewed my commitment to the Lord. Sometimes I was so overwhelmed with God and His beauty that I would actually yell, "Lord, you are amazing! Lord, thank you!" I'm no charismatic, and as far as I know, no one else heard me yelling except God (and maybe Dave.) If someone else heard me, then they heard someone in the middle of the wilderness glorifying the Lord. Think about it, the Lord saved me, delivered my soul and gave me hope. Love for Him should cause me to earnestly desire to glorify Him out of my intense passion for Him. And sometimes, when I think I'm all alone in the wilderness, why not shout it out? Communing with Him on a hike without distractions is one thing, but doing it daily throughout a busy and hectic life is another. But that is the aim. For He is worthy.

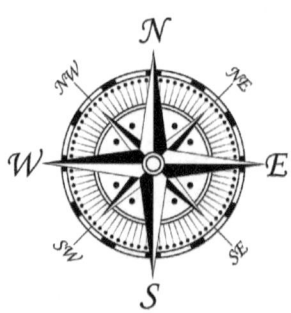

Faith Principle 2
Abel: The faithful worship God from the heart

True faithfulness has to begin in the heart. If the heart is right, then the right God-honoring actions will naturally flow forth. If the heart isn't true, then whatever the external results mean nothing. We can fool people, but God sees the heart, and God is never fooled. Abel shows us how important it is to have a right heart if you are going to live out your faith in a way that truly pleases God. Verse 4 of Hebrews 11 shows us this, "By faith Abel offered to God a more excellent sacrifice than Cain, through which he obtained witness that he was righteous, God testifying of his gifts; and through it he being dead still speaks."

In this verse, we see the first personal example of someone who lived by faith—Abel. His faith was tangibly seen because he gave a more excellent sacrifice to God than his brother Cain did. Abel lived by faith while Cain did not.

This takes us back to what happened in Genesis 4:1-5. Verses 1-2 says, "Now Adam knew Eve his wife, and she conceived and bore Cain, and said, 'I have acquired a man from the Lord.' Then she bore again, this time his brother Abel. Now Abel was a keeper of sheep, but Cain was a tiller of the ground."

Think about the context of what is happening here. Adam and Eve lost paradise and now sin has entered in, and everything is different. No more Eden, no more walking with God in the garden, no more innocence, no more perfect marriage, no more perfect anything. Instead, they now find themselves driven out of the garden of Eden and beginning their slow decay towards death.

But as the text says, in the course of time as Adam and Eve struggled to survive in the newly fallen world, they began to have children. But unlike their parents who were created without sin, the children of Adam and Eve are born with sinful natures. Verse 1 says that Eve bore Cain, and then verse 2 tells us that Adam and Eve had another baby boy named Abel.

Cain literally means *gotten* or *I have acquired*.[18] The name Abel means *vapor, vanity, a mere breath*.[19] This name expresses the brevity of life. We don't know how long he actually lived because Genesis doesn't say, but measured against the long-life spans before the flood, where people lived for hundreds and hundreds of years because of the nature of the world before the flood, Abel's life was very short.

Verse 2 tells us more about Cain and Abel. They have now grown up and are men. Abel was a keeper of sheep, while Cain was a tiller of the ground. These are honorable professions, and both are important for helping their family survive in the newly fallen world. So far things are looking good. Two sons, both doing noble and important jobs, and proud parents. But then look what happened. Verse 3, "And in the process of time it came to pass that Cain brought an offering of the fruit of the ground to the Lord. Abel also brought of the firstborn of his flock and of their fat. And the Lord respected Abel and his offering, but he did not respect Cain and his offering, and Cain was very angry, and his countenance fell."

This is interesting. That phrase "in the process of time" is indefinite. In other words, we don't know how much time has passed or how old Cain and Abel were at this point. This could have been a few years, a few decades, or even a hundred years down the line, we don't know. We just know that it happened.

What happened? Both Cain and Abel brought an offering to the Lord, which was an act of worship. This was a way for them to honor God; it was a way for them to show respect and adoration to the living God who created them. The Hebrew term for both Cain's and Abel's offering is the

---

[18] Francis Brown, S.R Driver, & Charles Briggs, *Enhanced Brown-Driver-Briggs Hebrew and English Lexicon*, (Oxford: Clarendon Press, 1977), 884.
[19] Ibid, 210.

term *minha* which can be either a general term for *offering, gift, present, or tribute*, or else it can be a specialized term for a *grain offering*.[20] So they came bringing their offerings to God to honor Him, to pay tribute to Him as the giver of all things, to give Him a gift because they want to glorify Him. Or so it seemed. I believe this wasn't the first time that they did this, rather, this was a regular practice for them as a way to give honor and glory to the Lord.

Although the Bible doesn't tell us this, I think it's likely God had revealed to them that this was an important way to show their worship, love, and reverence to God; by giving something to Him. This makes sense, because one important way we show our worship, love, adoration, gratitude, and thanks to God is by giving offerings to Him. Be it money, service, gifts, talents, time, or something else, based on our love for Him. So, Cain and Abel were worshipping God by this offering, and I have no doubt that they knew what God desired for them to give. I also believe God had told them specific ways they were to bring these offerings, which reveals why Abel's was accepted and why Cain's wasn't. They certainly knew what God wanted from them.

So first, Cain brought an offering to the Lord. This offering consisted of the fruit of the ground. Where did he bring this offering? The text doesn't say, but it undoubtedly was a place that had been set up for that very purpose. So he brought his grain, the fruit of the ground, and he gave it as an offering to the Lord.

Next came Abel, and Abel's offering consisted of one of the firstborns of his flock, most likely a lamb. Notice that Abel brought the firstborn, and also notice he brought the firstborn of the flock and of their fat. This is a way of saying that Abel brought the best before the Lord and offered it up to Him. So, he brought animals, and not just animals, but the fattest

---

[20] *TWOT*, 1042.

of the firstborn, the best of the best. Notice that it doesn't say anything like this about Cain's offering. So Abel brought the fattest and the first, while Cain simply brought an offering. That's a big difference, because if Cain had brought the best then it probably would have told us that he had brought the first fruits. But it doesn't say that. No, Cain simply brought an offering.

God recognized the difference because the end of verse 4 says the Lord respected Abel and his offering, but he didn't respect Cain and his offering. That word *respect* means to regard, to accept, or to pay attention to, and this tells us that the Lord was pleased with Abel's offering while He wasn't pleased with Cain's.[21] How exactly did they know whose offering was accepted and whose was rejected? It doesn't say, but however this happened, they knew. Perhaps fire came down and devoured Abel's offering and not Cain's. However, it happened, there was no doubt about what God thought of each offering. God respected Abel's and not Cain's.

There are basically two lines of thought when considering why the Lord regarded Abel's offering and not Cain's. First, many believe the reason is simple; because Abel gave the best while Cain didn't, and the text is clear about that fact. Abel was presenting this offering to God from his heart, while Cain was doing it out of mere duty. Abel's offering was out of faith and love for God, while Cain was doing it simply to get through it. This is apparent. That Cain is going through the religious motions; that Cain was doing the duty without the love. Cain is therefore the first Pharisee, he's a faker, he's wearing a spiritual mask, and God sees right through it. Abel's offering was done with a desire to worship God from the heart, in spirit and in truth. Cain's token was the effort of dead and empty religion. But did he really think he could fool God, the God who sees the heart?

---

[21] Ibid, 944.

Proverbs 5:21 says, "For the ways of man are before the eyes of the Lord, and God ponders all his paths." Proverbs 21:2 says, "Every way of a man is right in his own eyes, but the Lord weighs the heart." That doesn't bode well for Cain who had spiritual heart issues, because the Bible is very clear that first and foremost, God wants our hearts. He wants us to love Him from our hearts, He wants us to be captivated by Him, He wants us to be lost in wonder, love, and praise to Him, He wants us to obey Him from a heart that is intensely in love with Him, and the last thing He wants is empty ritual, duty without heart, or offerings without love—like that of Cain.

But then there's another thought regarding Cain's offering and why it wasn't acceptable to God. Notice that Abel brought an animal sacrifice to God while Cain didn't. Some believe that this was the real issue.[22] In Genesis 3:21, God killed an innocent animal that was guilty of nothing, which was the first death ever, in order to clothe and cover sinful Adam and Eve with garments of animal skins. This is a beautiful picture of Christ and what He would do for believing sinners throughout history. The picture is one of God covering the naked sinner with a garment of righteousness, with a garment of salvation through the sacrifice of an innocent victim, of a substitute dying for the guilty, of a sacrifice on the behalf of another.[23] What a picture of Jesus, who died as the lamb slain from before the foundation of the world. For by his death the believing sinner is covered; by His death the believing sinner is atoned for. And so right from the beginning, there is a foreshadowing of Christ and what He would do for all who believe.

---

[22] James Montgomery Boice, *Genesis: Vol. 1, an Expositional Commentary*, (Baker Books: Grand Rapids, MI, 1998), 251.
[23] Ibid.

Many scholars think that with this picture of a substitutionary death in place already (Genesis 3:21), that God had communicated that this is the kind of sacrifice that He wanted from his people, specifically from Cain and Abel. Where you approach God realizing that you deserve death for your sin, and you recognize that by offering a sacrifice in death, that it serves as a wonderful symbol of the need for a substitute who can die in your place by which your sin can be covered through faith in God. Of course, this was to be done with the right heart and attitude of love, faith, and devotion to the Lord. Abel did this and Cain didn't, and many believe that this is the real reason why God rejected Cain's offering; because it wasn't an animal sacrifice done in repentant faith.

Some might be skeptical about this view, but the writer of Hebrews has something to say about it. In Hebrews 12:24 it says, "You have come to Jesus, the mediator of the New Covenant, and to the blood of sprinkling that speaks better things than that of Abel." This is interesting, because here, the writer of Hebrews is talking about Abel's offering, and then about Christ and what He did for us. This shows us that Abel's offering wasn't just an offering, but it had to do with his sin and with a substitutionary death on the behalf of another. The point is that while Abel's offering couldn't truly atone for his sin, it was a picture of the one sacrifice that could—Jesus Christ on the cross. And when Abel offered that animal in faith, realizing his sin, realizing his need for covering, for grace, for forgiveness from God—that sacrifice done in faith allowed his sin to be rolled forward and placed onto Christ who could pay the penalty of death once and for all, not only for Abel but for all who believe. And so, there is validity to this second view.

It shows us that Abel understood things. He understood his sin, his need for covering, his need for forgiveness and his need for God's grace. His offering reflected that reality. So again, Abel gave the fattest and the best. Abel gave in faith. Abel gave out of his love for the Lord, and he sought to honor Him from the heart. Cain didn't do any of that. The encouragement here is to be like Abel; to be faithful like Abel was faithful, and to show forth your faith like Abel did.

Notice a few things here about Abel. First, he was righteous. "He obtained witness (testimony, commendation) that he was righteous." What does this mean? First of all, Scripture teaches that God alone justifies and declares sinners as righteous by their faith, and not by their works. This is a judicial action where God acquits the guilty sinner on the basis of Christ's death which satisfied the penalty that the sinner deserves. At the moment of true faith, God credits the penalty of our sin to Christ, and then he credits the righteousness of Christ to us. Once the sinner has trusted in Jesus Christ as Lord and Savior in saving repentant faith, his or her life will then reflect that saving faith with a progressively growing God-centered life; of a faith-filled life that consists of battling sin, pleasing God and walking faithfully.

This is what we know: Abel was righteous before God, he was right with God, He believed in God in saving faith that led him to offer up this acceptable sacrifice to the Lord. Note that he wasn't righteous because he offered this sacrifice, but he offered this sacrifice because he was righteous. He loved God from the heart, and that led him to show it with acceptable sacrifices to the Lord.

The same is true with us today, the only difference is now that Christ has come, our sacrifices are spiritual sacrifices, not animal sacrifices. Our sacrifices that please God consist of our hearts and our lives lived out faithfully as a daily offering up to Him. Because we love Him, we give, we serve, we fight sin, and we pursue the things that honor our God. Abel did it with his life and then with his animal sacrifice, and we do it with our lives and with our spiritual sacrifices. God is pleased with offerings like this. The faithful offer up offerings to God like Abel.

Notice that God testified of his gifts. In verse 2 it says, "For by it, the elders obtained a good testimony," and Abel is one of those who obtained a good testimony from the Lord. The word "testimony" is from the Greek word *marturion* from which we get the word martyr. It means to "bear witness and to testify to."[24] Here, we see that God testified to Abel's gifts, sacrifices, and offerings. In other words, God was well pleased. God approved, and that's amazing.

The world often ridicules or despises the person who lives by faith. But so what, as long as God approves. Abel's offering made his brother mad, but so what, as long as God approves. Abel's offering brought about his death, but so what, as long as God approves. Nothing is more important than pleasing God, and nothing is more valuable than the approval of God. Even if it means that other people don't like you, and even if faithfully honoring God brings about your death. One is temporary and the other is eternal. The wise Christians are those who live faithfully each day to seek God's approval, God's positive testimony. Abel is a great example for us today because he lived out his faith even when it came with a price, for the faithful know that nothing is more important than pleasing and honoring God in this fading life, for that lasts forever.

Notice also that Abel still speaks to us today, even though he's dead. That's incredible! Don't you want your faithful life to speak to generations, years down the line, long after you are dead? Having a faith like Abel's that flows from the heart and that obeys accordingly, does that.

Do you remember what happened to Abel? Genesis 4:5-8 gives us the details:

> And Cain was very angry, and his countenance fell. So the Lord said to Cain, 'Why are you angry? And why has your countenance

---

[24] Kittel, 564.

> fallen? If you do well, will you not be accepted? And if you do not do well, sin lies at the door. And its desire is for you, but you should rule over it.' Now Cain talked with Abel his brother; and it came to pass, when they were in the field, that Cain rose up against Abel his brother and killed him.

How incredibly sad is this? Do you see what Cain did here? He was trying to fashion a god into his own image, but the one true God doesn't like that and He won't play those foolish games. So Cain is now angry because God accepted Abel's offering and rejected his own. God even warned him, but Cain didn't repent, and now, the sin that was crouching at the door, has kicked the door in. Note that sin will do that every time if we don't repent and go to God with it.

Notice here that sin is depicted like a beast of prey, like a ravenous lion. It's waiting, it's crouching, and it's ready to pounce and seize its opportunity. This shows us how sin is always lurking, and how it never gives in, it never sleeps, and it is always right around the corner, waiting for us to give it an opening. Sin is relentless, and when you give it even a tiny opening, it runs through that opening every time. Sin is like a tidal wave, or like a fire that quickly grows out of control, or like a teddy bear that turns into a grizzly. God warned Cain about this, but instead of repenting, he held on to the anger.

Now what? Murder. Cain talked with Abel his brother, and this is a set up. The way the Hebrew language is written brings out the fact that Cain is basically luring Abel out into the field so he can then kill him. I can hear him, "Hey, Abel, let's go for a walk in the field. Let's talk. We haven't spoken very much lately so let's do some brotherly bonding." He flattered with the lips while he had murder on his heart. In whatever way this happened, it is clear that Cain spoke to Abel, and they then went out into the field and Abel never came back. This is cold and calculated. This is not some accident; it's violent, vicious, premeditated and wicked. The word *brother* is used twice in this verse which emphasizes the closeness and intimacy of Abel to Cain. Think about that. This is the brother that he grew up with when there was no one else around. This is his own flesh and blood. Even so, Cain lures his brother out into the field, he then rises up against him, and he kills him. The first human death ever.

The good news is that the first one that dies is a believer, and so when he died, he went right into the presence of the Lord. Note also that the first person to die is a martyr. For Abel died for his faith, for obeying God, for doing the will of God and for giving a pleasing offering to the Lord. Sometimes pleasing God has dire consequences in this life, but it has unbounding blessings in the next.

How did Cain murder Abel? We don't know, but it's ugly, brutal, evil, and wretched. And so we find that the first death in the Bible is also the first murder in the Bible, and it didn't take long. At the end of verse 8, the word *killed* is a common word in the Old Testament for intentional murder.[25] In 1 John 3:12 it says, "Cain, who was of the evil one, slew his brother. And for what reason did he slay him? Because his deeds were evil, and his brothers were righteous." So this murder was done out of jealousy, it was done because Abel's righteousness became intolerable to Cain, and it was done because Cain was harboring jealousy, anger and hatred in his heart.

But what about Abel who is our faithful example? He is fine and good. Abel never lived in Eden, but the minute he died, he went to heaven forever. So there are no worries at all for Abel. He still speaks to us today. How? His faithful life. Interestingly, we have no recorded words that Abel spoke, and yet thousands of years after his death, he still speaks. This shows us the power of a faithful and godly life. It can not only impact your

---

[25] BDB, 247.

generation, but it can also have an impact for many successive generations. What then is the call? To live faithfully by worshiping God from the heart. When you do that, it will compel you to do what God calls you to do even if your brother does the opposite. It will compel you to obey God even when there is a price to be paid for your obedience. It will compel you to live out your faith tangibly even in the midst of opposition. The faithful understand this, and their lives reveal this.

Viewed from his lifetime, Abel's life seems wasted. Think about it. He died young and without accomplishing much of anything. But numerous generations have looked at his faith and learned that even if we suffer and die for the cause of righteousness, it isn't in vain. Cain on the other hand, seems to have lived a long and relatively prosperous life on earth. He built cities and fathered many children who were successful in worldly terms. But Cain's life was the wasted one. Abel was the true success, and the actions of simple faithful worship to God from the heart inspire us today. Be like Abel. The faithful are captivated from the heart with God. They love Him, and their love shows itself with a faithful life, even when it comes with a price. The faithful battle rote religion, cold ritual, going through the motions without heart, and hypocritical external empty religious ritual. The faithful love God from the heart, and their lives show that love in their actions. Like Abel.

CHAPTER 4

John Muir Trail:

One of the good things about my John Muir Trail hike was my conversations with Dave. Even though we hiked separately during much of the day, there were numerous times when we hiked together. We usually started the mornings early, hiking together in the dark for the first hour before Dave's faster pace carried him forward. Around lunchtime, after waiting for me to catch up on the trail, we'd again hike at my pace for a while. It was during these times, and at night as we settled around camp and ate dinner where we had wonderful times of encouragement in the Lord. Our conversations were times when we could build each other up to stay faithful and to continue to live for the glory and pleasure of God. Don't kid yourself, pastors need this type of encouragement just as much as anyone else. There is so much in life that can bring discouragement: job, worries, concerns for our children, health issues, sin issues and so on—it can all become incredibly disheartening. During those times, we would remind each other of what really mattered, what the real aim in life is as a Christian, and we would encourage each other to fight against life's distractions that block us from glorifying God.

On our fourth day, we got lost. We'd just finished a long trek uphill when we saw a stream where we could refill our water bottles. We had another long uphill climb ahead of us and when we returned to the main trail we went to the left, which looked to be the correct way. Evidently, we weren't the only people to have made this mistake. We followed a cleared trail as it curved uphill for a bit and then plunged down a steep path over some boulders to a trail below. It was sketchy. We thought, "This can't be the trail, it's too steep and dangerous." We retraced our steps to make sure we hadn't missed something (without looking at the map). No, this was the right way, it had to be. We went down the steep trail. It was exhausting and treacherous. It became so steep that we removed our packs and lowered them down separately to get to the bottom. Once at the bottom, the trail continued off to the right for a few yards where it fizzled into a dead end. It was only then that we knew we had made a mistake. We turned and looked at the trail we'd just come down. The slope ahead of us was heartbreaking. It was midday and I was already beat. The uphill climb over the rocks was incredibly tiring. By the time we got back to where we had veered off the trail, we had lost more than an hour. Dave then looked at the map, which clearly went off to the right. The path was hidden by a big boulder. Once we saw what the map told us, we went by the boulder and the trail was clearly marked out for us. Dumb.

That night's conversation was minimal, we were both so tired. But it had a theme we kept the rest of our journey: stay on the path, keep going, consult the map, don't quit and encourage each other regularly. Dave helped me to get back on the path of the JMT, and he encouraged me to stay faithful and please God in my spiritual life. One is temporary, and one is eternal.

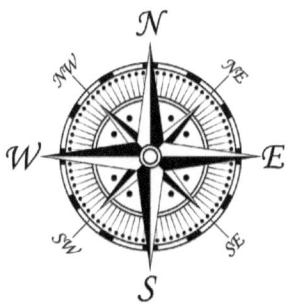

Faith Principle 3
Enoch: The faithful live to please God

Pleasing God should be the Christian's greatest joy. The faithful are those who live for the pleasure of God. Verse 5 gives us another example of what true faith should look like in the example of Enoch:

> By faith Enoch was taken away so that he did not see death, "and was not found, because God had taken him"; for before he was taken he had this testimony, that he pleased God.

Here we see that Enoch is given to us as an example of faith. What is it about Enoch's faith that should encourage and inspire us? He pleased God. Genesis 5:21-24 gives us more information:

> Enoch lived sixty-five years, and begot Methuselah. After he begot Methuselah, Enoch walked with God three hundred years, and had sons and daughters. So all the days of Enoch were three

> hundred and sixty-five years. And Enoch walked with God; and he was not, for God took him.

What do we know about Enoch? We know that his father's name was Jared, and his son's name was Methuselah. We also know that he had other sons and daughters, and that he lived for 365 years. This was a relatively short life compared to most of his contemporaries at that unique period of time—before the flood when people lived much longer than today, post-flood. We also know that Enoch walked with God, which is pointed out to us two times in the four verses of Genesis 5. So his walking with God is the thing that enabled him to please God.

What else do we know about this man? That one-day Enoch was, and then the next day he was not. In other words, Enoch did not see death. As opposed to dying, God simply took him home. Can you imagine what that was like? Enoch was one of only two men ever who have escaped physical death—the other being Elijah who was taken up to heaven in a chariot of fire in a whirlwind. So amazingly, Enoch is a man who'd escaped death and who went straight to heaven.

Why did God do this to Enoch? It seems clear that it was because Enoch pleased God and walked with Him. How long did he walk with and please God? Well, it was three hundred years before God took him. Think about that. Not twenty years, not fifty years, and not seventy years but three hundred years. What was that like? We can only wonder. Try to think about the Godliest old saint you know, and then add to that person's life between two hundred and two hundred-fifty more years of spiritual growth and passion for God. That's Enoch. Three hundred years of battling against the world, the flesh and the devil. Three hundred years of faithful service to the Lord. Three hundred years of spiritual growth. Enduring life for three hundred years is one thing, but then, to think that this man remained dedicated, devoted, loyal and faithful to God through it all is truly amazing. And then one day God decided to take this saint home without facing death.

Enoch is used as an example of faith for us. The desire? Have a faith that pleases God and that walks with Him like Enoch. And then think about this: since we only have a few years compared to Enoch, that's all the more reason to please and walk with God faithfully. At the most, I will only have thirty more years to please God with this fading life. I had better redeem every day and live faithfully for His glory while I am still able. Enoch challenges all of us to do that. He walked with God for three hundred years. Surely, we can do it for fifty, or for thirty, or for ten, or for this next year.

The call then is to faithfully walk with God every day. Or in context of Hebrews 11, to have this testimony: he pleased God. True faith lives for the pleasure of God and Enoch understood that. Even before the flood, this man knew what mattered most. As we stand this side of the cross, how much more us today?

Colossians 1:10 says, "And we pray this in order that you may live a life worthy of the Lord and may please him in every way: bearing fruit in every good work, growing in the knowledge of God." Life is about pleasing Him. Galatians 1:10 says, "Am I now trying to win the approval of men, or of God? Or am I trying to please men? If I were still trying to please men, I would not be a servant of Christ." Life is not about pleasing men and it's not about pleasing yourself, but instead, life is about pleasing, glorifying and serving the Lord in every way, wherever you find yourself.

As Alexander MacLaren said:

> You report to headquarters. Never mind what anybody else thinks of you. Your business is to please the Lord, and the less you

> trouble yourselves about pleasing men, the more you will succeed in pleasing Him.[26]

That's true whether you were living before the flood or whether you're alive and well today, the goal hasn't changed. Please God. Glorify God. Honor your king. This is indeed the chief aim of man, and this is what the faithful do. Is it your chief aim? If not, then you're wasting your life. Please don't waste your one life, because while you may not live for a long time like Enoch, who knows if your life will be cut short like Abel? The wise soul is the one who pleases God today, because tomorrow we might be gone. The ones who live by faith earnestly seek to please God like Enoch.

Faith Principle 4
The faithful diligently seek God

Notice what the writer of Hebrews says in verse 6. "But without faith it is impossible to please Him, for he who comes to God must believe that He is, and that He is a rewarder of those who diligently seek Him." Here we see that you can't please God without faith. Faith is the key. The writer uses strong words here. "Without faith it's impossible to please God." *Impossible* speaks of being powerless and incapable.[27] This means only true believers can please God, and therefore, non-believers aren't capable of truly pleasing God. Why? Because they place their faith in something else, something less, something that is temporary, fading and meaningless in the end. That is offensive to the God who created them. Everyone in

---

[26] Alexander Maclaren, *Expositions of Holy Scripture: 2 Corinthians*, (Grand Rapids, MI: Eerdmans, 1944), 156.
[27] Louw, 668.

history has put their faith in something, but it's only those who put their faith in God who are well pleasing to Him. Like Enoch.

The word *please* means to give pleasure or satisfaction.[28] The idea is to excite agreeable emotions in another, and here, in the Lord God Almighty. That's amazing. We can please God as we live out our faith. So to call is to be like Enoch and live out your faith with passion. If you love someone, you aim to please him or her. Faith pleases God. The greatest commandment is that we should love the Lord our God with all of our heart, soul, mind, and strength, and a faith lived out is a great way we show that love to Him.

Notice that in verse 6, the writer says that to come to God, you have to believe that He is. That is the foundation. When the author says we must believe "God is," he means we must believe that God is exactly who His Word reveals Him to be, and not who we conceive Him to be—and that's a big difference.[29] I've heard it many times, people say, "My God is a God of love not a God of judgment." Then your god is a false god, a figment, a made-up god. "My God is tolerant, and He doesn't care how you choose to live your life so long as you are happy." Then your God is a fraud who can't save your soul. "My God can be found by many different paths so long as you are sincere in the path you take." Then you have a fake god because that is not the God of the Bible. We don't make the rules, God does, and God shows us what those rules are in His Word. We don't fit Him into our box; we need to fit into His. He's the authority, not us. And so, to believe in God as you conceive Him to be is to believe in an idol, a god of your own making and imagination, which is satanic.

In Exodus 32, we find the incident of the golden calf. If you remember, the children of Israel had been in bondage in Egypt for more than four-

---

[28] Kittel, 186.
[29] Ibid, 206.

hundred years. God called Moses and told him that He had heard their cries, and He was about to deliver them. To help Moses prove the existence and power of God, Moses was given a number of miraculous signs, including ten plagues to help the Israelites believe and be set free. After the plagues, the Israelites came out of Egypt with a renewed belief in the God of their fathers. They passed through the Red Sea on dry land while the Egyptian army drowned, and they were brought to the mountain of God to receive His law.

While Moses was on the mountain, the people grew anxious down on the plain. Moses spent forty days on the mountain with God, and by the end of that time the people had given up on Moses, thinking he'd died or had left them. The people then urged Aaron, their temporary leader, to make gods for them to follow after and worship. And so, Aaron took their gold earrings which they had brought from Egypt, and he melted them down to make a golden idol. The idol he crafted for them was a calf. But notice that Aaron maintained the name of the Lord in connection with that calf. He said in Exodus 32:5, "This is your god O Israel that brought you out of the land of Egypt." Oh no it wasn't. It was earrings not Yahweh. The people then offered sacrifices, and they worshiped this new false god.

This is exactly what people are doing today. They claim, "I'm a Christian; I believe in God; I love my God." But the god they love looks nothing like the God of the Bible, the one true God. Therefore, their god is a made-up god, it's just *earrings* that they call god. It's not the God of the Bible. Why do people do this? Because we want things our way, we want our sin, and we don't like to submit even when heaven and hell hang in the balance.

God wasn't happy with the Israelites and He's not happy with those today who fashion their fake gods. God held Israel accountable for their sin, just as He holds us all accountable for our sin today. People respond, "But I'm good; I deserve to go to heaven." That's a golden calf religion, for no one is good enough for heaven on their own. They say, "But I'm sincere." That's a golden calf false religion, for there are many who are sincerely wrong who have denied the truth of the Bible. Sincerity alone can't save anyone. "I just don't feel like God should tell me how to live my life." Your feelings betray you. Basing your eternal fate on your fleeting feelings is a golden calf religion that has led many to hell. To be saved, you need to have true faith in the God of the Bible and in His message of salvation by grace through faith alone. The faithful then seek to please this amazing God.

A couple of years ago, the specialty/import store, Cost Plus World Market, launched a promotion over the holidays. I found the promotion both fascinating and a little bit addicting for me. In this campaign, the store management would hide five little cardboard cards with a picture of a golden Llama on each. The cards depicted a monetary reward, ranging from $10 to $50. The rules stated that once a person found a golden Llama card and won, they couldn't win again during that promotion period.

When I heard about this from my wife, I grew really excited. I love a good hunt. Each day, through a software application, Cost Plus World Market offered a different clue about where the llamas were hidden—next to something blue, by something metal, something clear, etc. This made it even more challenging to me. My wife's goal would be to find the llama to save money while shopping. My goal was the find the llama. The savings was nice, but it was the searching and the finding that I liked the most.

We went on a Saturday morning and we arrived before the store opened. My wife had the store's app on her cell phone so we knew that day's clue. A crowd of early shoppers began to form but it didn't matter, we were the first in line and we were ready—when the doors opened, I would go right, she would go left. Finally, the doors unlocked, and the search was on.

Come to find out, I have an amazing gift. I am good at finding golden llamas. That first day, I found three llamas. I took one, I gave one to my wife, and I gave one to my wife's friend. I was upset that I didn't find the other two. Over the next couple of weeks, I returned to the store and found golden llamas for everyone in my family, many of my friends and a surprising number of complete strangers. They were grateful to me because I saved them some money, but again, my true aim wasn't really to save anyone money, it was to find the llama. Sometimes I would go to the store, search intently through the merchandise on display, find a llama or two without telling anyone and then leave. Why? Because it was the searching and the finding that mattered.

The first time the store ran the promotion, it culminated on Thanksgiving Day. They launched an identical promotion in December, and thus the cycle began again. I don't know why I got so caught up with finding those golden llamas. But to me, there was something exciting about searching for something so keenly and finding it. I'd found that most people didn't diligently seek the golden llama, but instead, if they sought it at all, they did so way too casually. As a result, they never found one. They weren't really committed; they only scanned. Few moved anything out of the way and even fewer were willing to stoop down to look, let alone get on their hands and knees to look—like I did. Also, most people weren't willing to put in the time needed to find a golden llama. Some would quit after only a few minutes of looking. While this might allow an occasional person to get lucky and find one, the golden llamas were usually found by those who were committed to finding them, those who were willing to put in the time to find them—again, like me.

The whole thing became quite a problem for me since I didn't have a ton of free time to make my way to Cost Plus World Market in the middle of the day and diligently apply myself to finding golden llamas. But it was sure fun.

My commitment to finding golden llamas is a bit of a ridiculous example of how the faithful are called to live: as diligent seekers, as those who are truly committed, as those who are willing to do whatever it takes to find what they are seeking. Golden llamas are one thing, but God's glory is quite another.

Verse 6 goes on and tells us that true faith in God diligently seeks Him. You believe in what He says, you put your faith in Him, and you entrust your soul into His hands. And then you must act because love compels you. *Seek* is an interesting word, and even though the word *diligent* isn't in the Greek, it's definitely implied. *Seek* is in the present tense, so we seek Him until we find Him, and then we keep on seeking Him. *Seek* means to search out with care, to inquire about, to investigate and to be intent on.[30] We seek Him first when we trust in Him in repentant faith for forgiveness and eternal life. But then after that, we keep on seeking Him by aiming at giving Him the glory in our lives, and by making Him the great object for which we live. This is what the writer of Hebrews is speaking of here in verse 6: now that we belong to Him, in faith we keep on seeking Him and His pleasure in our lives. This is what the faithful do because we love Him.

In faith, we diligently seek Him. This means that we stop looking at other things to satisfy us, and we look to Him alone. We look for Him to be our primary focus and first priority. It's the same thing as what the Apostle Paul said in Philippians 3:10: "I want to know him, and the power of His resurrection, and the fellowship of His sufferings, being made like Him in His death." In other words, I just want Him; more of Him. It's the same thought that King David expressed in Psalm 27:4: "One thing have I desired of the LORD, not two but one, that will I seek after; that I may dwell in the house of the LORD all the days of my life, to behold the beauty of the LORD, and to enquire in his temple." So, here's the idea: all

---

[30] Bauer, 338.

I want is Him, all I seek is Him. He is my life's passion because He is all that matters. Or as David said in Psalm 42:1-2, "As the deer pants after the water brooks, so pants my soul after thee, O God. My soul thirsts for God, for the living God: when shall I come and appear before God?" In other words, I pant for Him, I hunger for Him, I can't wait to see Him, and until I do, I'll look to Him as my all in all, my passion, my aim and my life. For who is greater than Him, and who is more worthy than Him? Nothing is close, and so, in faith, I diligently seek Him every day.

Psalm 27:8 says, "When you Lord said, 'Seek My face.' My heart said to You, 'Your face, Lord, I will seek.'" This is what the faithful do. What are you seeking today? Think about this: who or what else is more worthy of you diligently seeking after with your one life that you have? Is that other person more valuable than God; the God who can save your desperate soul? Is that drug more valuable than God? Is that thing more valuable than God who alone saves? Is your acceptance by your peers more valuable than God? Is that sin more valuable than God? Did your house die on a cross to save you from hell? Did any other person die on a cross to save you from hell? Did that drug or anything or anyone else besides Christ die on a cross to save your soul from hell? Who deserves our hearts more than God? Who is going to love you more than Him? Who has more compassion than Him? Who has more mercy, forgiveness and grace than Him? So why then would we diligently seek after lesser things?

Note also that true faith that diligently seeks God will be rewarded by Him. "He is the *rewarder* of those who diligently seek Him." The writer here is talking to Christians, and he is encouraging us to faithful living that bears much fruit, that abounds in good and Godly works because of our faith. It's not the reward of salvation, which is truly amazing, but it's the reward that comes on top of that, to those who bear much fruit for the glory of God.

This is truly amazing. Those who seek God out for salvation will be rewarded with eternal life. Note that the Bible tells us that those who seek God out for salvation by calling on Him for forgiveness and life were first sought out by God. No one can seek God in this manner unless He first seeks them out and awakens their dead-in-sin hearts. All those who call out to God in true faith will receive the reward of heaven and eternal glory. On top of that, we also know that God rewards faithfulness in the life of the Christian. Once you understand you are saved through His grace, you then diligently seek to glorify Him every day, knowing that it pleases Him and will be rewarded by Him. In 2 Cor. 5:9-10 it says this:

> Therefore, whether present or absent, we make it our aim to be well-pleasing to God. Why? For we all must appear before the judgment seat of Christ, that each one may receive the things done in the body, according to what he has done, whether good or bad.

What does this mean? This judgment is for the Christian, and it is speaking of a judgment of evaluation for the Christian for how he lived out his faith. In other words, it's a judgment of the works of the Christian, the fruit of the Christian. The phrase, judgment seat, *bema* in the Greek, literally means *step*, as in a raised platform or seat.[31] This was where a Roman magistrate sat to act as a judge. The bema seat was an object of reverence and fear for all the people, especially for those who stood before it. A person who stood before this bema seat would have his or her deeds examined for the purpose of either indicting them or for rewarding them. In the same manner, we as Christians will stand before God and give an accounting for how we lived out our faith. Note that this is not a

---

[31] Colin Brown, *Dictionary of New Testament Theology*, vol 2, (Grand Rapids, MI: Zondervan, 1986), 369.

judgment for sin since every sin of every believer was judged at the cross when God punished Jesus for all that sin in our place. Also, this is not a judgment of condemnation because Romans 8:1 tells us, "There is therefore now no condemnation to those who are in Christ Jesus." Instead, this is simply a judgment of evaluation and eternal rewards.[32] So as Christians, we are already saved by grace through faith in Christ and we no longer stand condemned in our sin because of the cross. However, we will still be held accountable for how we lived out our faith. Therefore, it matters greatly how you live as a Christian, for it will be accounted for before the Lord and rewarded accordingly.

Note that every Christian will appear before this judgment seat, and no one will escape it. In other words, we will all give an accounting. In that day, the full truth about our lives, our morals and our deeds will be made clear. There, each will discover the real verdict of his life, of his ministry, of his service and of his motives. As John MacArthur says:

> All hypocrisy will be stripped away; all temporal matters with no eternal significance will vanish like wood, hay, and stubble, and only what is to be rewarded as eternally valuable will be left.[33]

This is good to know; that what we have done as Christians will be evaluated and rewarded. This means that it is possible to have a saved soul and a virtually wasted life, although it's not recommended. But more than that, this reality should be an encouragement in our service to the Lord. It should remind us of the principle in Hebrews 6:10, "For God is not unjust to forget your work and labor of love which you have shown toward His

---

[32] John MacArthur, *The MacArthur New Testament Commentary: 2 Corinthians*, (Chicago, IL: Moody Publishers, 2003), 178.
[33] Ibid.

name, in that you have ministered to the saints, and do minister." In other words, God sees all, God knows all, He knows your heart, He sees your Christians works, your sacrifices, your service, your faithfulness in action, and He will not forget. And when you stand before Him, He will not forget and He will reward it accordingly. What is that reward? I believe it's the good testimony from the Lord that is mentioned in verse 2. What could be better than that for us whose aim is to please and glorify God? It fits within the context, that those who live faithfully for the glory of God obtain a good testimony from Him, not only in this life, but also in the next when we finally get to see Him face to face. Can you picture it? We you declare, "Here Lord, I did it all for you." And our Lord will respond, "Well done, I am well pleased." Amazing.

So clearly, how you live out your faith matters greatly. Life is short, but diligently seeking and pleasing God in faith is eternal. What about you? What will you bring to Him on that day? Will you say, "Here Lord, here is my duffel bag." Or would you prefer to say, "Here Lord, here is my truck load. And another truck load is on the way."

Enoch pleased God and lived out his faith, and he diligently sought God and His glory in his life. The result? He didn't see death. This doesn't mean that every faithful God-pleaser will escape death, but it meant that for Enoch. What an amazing man he was. He loved God. He was a true believer who lived by faith. He pleased God with his three-hundred-and-sixty-year life, and he diligently and continually sought the Lord and His glory in his life. And on top of all of that, Jude 14 tells us that Enoch preached and warned people about the coming judgment in the midst of some very harsh circumstances.

And then one day boom, he was taken away by faith. The implication is that God wanted him because He pleased God so very much. Some commentators say that God took him because He didn't want him to get polluted by the corruptions of this world. That he had been so faithful for so many years that God just thought, "There's no sense in leaving a man like this in this world," and so He just took him on up. As Psalm 116:15 says, "Precious in the sight of the Lord is the death of his saints." Why? Because God loves His saints. And so God took him. I don't think God's going to take me like that, but isn't it great to know that how we live out our faith here can truly be well-pleasing to the God of all Creation?

Can't you picture his family around the dinner table that night. Someone asks, "Where is Enoch? What happened to Enoch? Why don't we see Enoch around anymore?"

Someone else answers, "God took him."

"Why?"

"His faith," the answer would come. "His faith that caused him to live radically for the pleasure of God."

I want to have a faith like that. It comes when we faithfully live for God's pleasure and lift Him high in our day-to-day lives. Ask, "Would this please God?" If not, then don't do it. If so, then do it. It's not rocket science, but it definitely takes focused faith in the living God who saved us. Wouldn't it be great if one day in the near future, where my three daughters are gathered around the dinner table, and one of them asks, "Hey mom, where's dad?"

CHAPTER 5

John Muir Trail:

Fifteen days on the trail can get mundane. The beauty makes it worth it along with finishing a hard task, but think about it; all you are doing all day is walking. After the third day, I was fed up with setting up camp at night and tearing it down in the morning. The last thing you want to do when you finish a long hike is to set up camp again. No, you want to eat something and then go to bed. You're hungry and exhausted, but you can't eat because you have things you have to do first. You have to set up camp. You have to get cleaned up in freezing cold water. You have to use the restroom, which isn't always easy or fun in the wilderness. You have to get your food and clothes organized for the next day, and so on. All of this has to be done before you can even think about eating. The mornings were especially brutal. Starting out, it was dark, and it would take me an hour to break camp—to wake up, get dressed, get packed up, get everything ready for the day, eat and then head out. By the end of the hike, I was able to cut it down to 45 minutes, but it wasn't easy, especially when all you wanted to do was stay in the warm sleeping bag. By the time I was done packing everything up for the day, I was already tired.

Then what? Walk. All day. Don't quit. Keep moving forward. The path is clear (most of the time), so stay on it and keep going. Simple but not easy. About halfway through the hike on the seventh day I felt a sharp pain in my knee as I was ascending one especially brutal pass. It hurt bad enough that I worried my hike could be coming to a quick end. I've had knee problems before, but I was hoping and praying that I would be okay on this hike. Wrong. I pushed through to the top of the pass where I hoped going downhill would ease the pain. I was wrong again. Going downhill only made things worse. I took a couple Advil, hoping that I would be able to make it down to Dave, where we had planned on making camp. I would tell him when I reached the site that I thought I was done. The pain shot through my knee with nearly every step going down the pass, I was miserable and relieved at the same time. The way I was processing this was that the throbbing in my knee would soon come to an end—as well, somewhere in the back of my head I knew that so to would the daily suffering of the hike. But to stop, I wouldn't reach my goal of finishing, let alone I'd lose the time I was having in the great beauty of the Sierras, communing with my God. It was bittersweet. As I hiked, I was surprised to find that the Advil was working. The pain had eased up. There was a hint of a thought that I might be able to continue. When I arrived at camp that night, I discussed things with Dave. We agreed to take it a day at a time. And that's what we did, for everyday left in the hike. The pain never really went away, but Advil in the morning and again in the afternoon helped me endure the pain and to keep hiking. One foot in front of the other, mile after mile, day after day to the end of the trail. Sometimes life is mundane and painful, but our call is to keep going and to never quit.

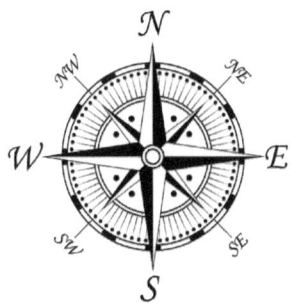

Faith Principle 5
Noah: The faithful fear God

As we have seen, the faithful lovers of God show forth their love and faith clearly. True faith must reveal itself with action, and the writer of Hebrews has been showing this fact to us. In Hebrews 11:7, we see another example of faithful living in Noah. Verse 7 says:

> By faith Noah, being divinely warned of things not yet seen, moved with godly fear, prepared an ark for the saving of his household, by which he condemned the world and became heir of the righteousness which is according to faith.

The call here is to have a faith like Noah. This takes us back to the sixth chapter of Genesis. At that time, there was great and wretched sin on the earth; sin so great that every intent in a man's heart was only evil continually, and so God was going to destroy the earth with a global flood. As Genesis 6:8-14a tells us:

> But Noah found grace in the eyes of the Lord. This is the genealogy of Noah. Noah was a just man, perfect in his generations. Noah walked with God. And Noah begot three sons: Shem, Ham, and Japheth. The earth also was corrupt before God, and the earth was filled with violence. So God looked upon the earth, and indeed it was corrupt; for all flesh had corrupted their way on the earth. And God said to Noah, "The end of all flesh has come before Me, for the earth is filled with violence through them; and behold, I will destroy them with the earth. Make yourself an ark of gopherwood..."

Grace in verse 8 means favor,[34] and *just* in verse 9 means justified,[35] showing us that Noah was a saved man; that Noah was declared to be righteous and right in the eyes of God. How did that happen? By grace through faith, for that is the only way a person can be justified and made right in the eyes of God as a sinful human being. And so, because Noah believed what God had revealed to him and had surrendered to the Lord in repentant faith, he was then saved from the just wages of his sin because of what Jesus would do years later on the cross. Noah looked forward to that perfect sacrifice to be seen in Jesus, and he appropriated that sacrifice by his faith.

Verse 9 in Genesis 6 also tells us that Noah was perfect in his generations. This doesn't mean that he was without sin, but it is a general description of this man of God in the midst of a sick and sin-filled world. The word *perfect* in the Hebrew means blameless, upright or whole,[36] and Noah was indeed a whole man in a broken world. The point is that when

---

[34] Brown, vol. 2, 115.
[35] Ibid, vol. 3, 352.
[36] BDB, 1071.

you saw Noah you saw a man of God, you saw a man who reflected the character of God, you saw a man who stood out and who rose above what was going on in the wretched sin-stained world around him. Think of it this way: everyone in the world was wicked continually, and against that backdrop stands this Godly man named Noah. In faith, Noah refused to let the crowd drag him down. Noah held strong even when he and his family were the only ones left who loved the Lord. Think of what that must have been like for him. Undoubtedly it meant persecution, mockery, ridicule and pressure. It certainly couldn't have been easy. For such singular righteousness and holiness would have been a constant affront to the culture around him.

Even so, Noah walked with God. As with Enoch, this describes a saved man who loved His Lord tangibly, wholeheartedly and fervently. Walking with God means that you love Him and that you want to serve Him. It means you want to honor Him, to please and glorify Him; you want to fight against the sin that battles against you because God hates sin and loves holiness. It means that you are growing to be more and more like Him and less like the ungodly world around you. It means that you put Him first above all else. It means that you give to Him and that you serve Him. You want to tell others about Him. You want to make Him your desire, your passion, your Lord and master. That was Noah. The call is to be faithful like him.

The narrative continues when God says, "Noah, I'm going to flood the world and I'm going to destroy everything, except for you, your family and some animals. Noah, build me an ark."

What did Noah do? In faith, he started building an ark. True faith obeys God like this. "God says it, I believe it and I will act on it—end of discussion." Note that Noah was clear that what he was hearing was the voice of God. Today God speaks to us in His written word, the Bible. But for Noah, in his unique time and situation before anything had ever been written, he heard God speak and it was clear to him. "God has spoken, and judgment is coming in the form of a flood. God told me to build an ark. Better get to building." And he did, for this is what real faith does. It takes God at His word. It trusts God's Word even when we don't fully understand it, and it hears the word of the unseen God regarding events that are not yet seen and brings them into present experience.

What else do we learn from Noah? We learn that he feared God. Verse 7 says that he was "moved by Godly fear." *Fear* here literally means to be concerned, to give heed to, and to be moved with regard, respect and reverence for someone—in this case, God.[37] And so Noah's faith in God's warning moved him to a reverential fear of God. He seemed to know that the God who spoke the universe into existence out of nothing is quite capable of commanding a flood to destroy all human life on earth. So, faith and fear go together. We trust God and we revere God. Faith motivates us, while reverential fear keeps us serious and mindful of the things of God.

The fear of God can be defined in this way: as a healthy respect and reverence for God, stemming from the knowledge of God, and resulting in obedience to God.[38] This fear and reverence stems from truly knowing Him; from understanding something of His greatness, power and holiness. Remember, our God is the eternal God who spoke the vastness of the universe into existence. We should have a healthy reverence for Him. We should especially fear Him when we realize that this great and powerful Creator is absolutely holy, and that we have violated His holy standards. He has mercifully made provision for our sins in the death of Christ, and

---

[37] W.E. Vine, *Vine's Expository Dictionary of Old and New Testament Words*, (Old Tappan, NJ: Fleming H. Revell Co, 1981), 84.
[38] Jerry Bridges, *The Joy of Fearing God*, (Colorado Springs, CO: Waterbrook Press, 1998), 25.

now He invites us to draw near to Him by grace through faith. But even so, we must always do so with reverence and awe because of who He is.

A proper fear of the Lord results in loving obedience to Him. If we're growing in the knowledge of God, we'll be growing in the fear of God, which means that we will flee sin and pursue the things that please Him. God sees, God knows, and God is worthy of a life of reverential fear and passionate love mixed together. Like Noah, if we have genuine faith in God, we will not only be moved by love in response to His great love, but we also will be moved by reverential fear in response to His holiness and His warnings of the judgment to come. Clearly Noah understood this. In faith, he listened to God, he revered God and then he obeyed God.

Faith Principle 6
The faithful obey God (Part I)

In what way did Noah obey God? In faith, he prepared an ark. This is difficult to imagine because Noah basically built an ocean liner in his backyard. It was 450-feet long, 75-feet wide, and 45-feet tall. Understand that this would have been all consuming for him for this didn't take just a few weeks or months. Incredibly, this took 120 years. Think about that: 120 years passed between when God told Noah to build the ark and when the actual floods came. And note this: it doesn't say that Noah ever heard back from God in those 120 years. He heard it, he feared God and he began building as well as preaching to the people, and 120 years later he's still building and preaching. That's amazing faith. Faith that we are called to have today.

Note that it had never rained on the earth up to that point. Instead, as Genesis 2:6 says, there was a mist that came up and watered the earth as opposed to rain like we have today. With the flood, the earth changed so that we now have rain. This makes what Noah did even more amazing.

"Noah, I'm going to flood the earth with rain."

There had to have been a puzzled look that crossed Noah's face. "Ummm, Lord, what's rain?"

"I'll show you in 120 years, just build the ark, okay?"

"Okay Lord, I trust You."

That's amazing faith. The ark was huge. It was basically an enormous box, but on top of building a huge box, Noah was also supposed to make rooms in the ark—thousands of rooms. On top of that, there were three levels on this ark. On top of that, Noah was supposed to cover the ark inside and outside with pitch. On top of that, he was supposed to make a window at the top of the ark as well as a door.

It has been calculated that the capacity of the ark was equivalent to 522 boxed cars. Now, years ago, somebody figured out that you could get 240 sheep in a boxed car. So, if you had 522 boxed cars with 240 sheep, you'd have a total of 125,000 animals. Sheep are probably larger than the average animal on the ark, and with that in mind, you had at least the space for 125,000 different animals.[39] According to calculations, the ark was large enough to carry two of every species of air breathing animal in the world today, and you could do it on half the deck space. The rest of the space would have been used for Noah and his family, as well as the other animals that were taken aboard for sacrificing and eating, storage and the like. The ark was certainly big enough. And one man built this amazing structure because God told him to build it. His faith in his good God compelled him to obey. That's what real faith does.

Think of the excuses that Noah and his wife could have used to argue with God: "It will be too expensive!"

"It's not reasonable!"

"It will take way too long!"

---

[39] Henry Morris, *The Genesis Record*, (Grand Rapids, MI: Baker Book house, 1976), 181.

"How will I be able to support my family while I'm building this thing?"

"A boat that size will never float."

"There's no way we will be able to fit in all those animals, and how will we get them here?"

Noah set aside all those excuses and he faithfully persevered in obedience until it was done. Noah did according to all that the Lord had commanded him. Oh, that we would have an obedient faith like Noah's.

The result: in faith, Noah built a ship in his backyard. His faith cost him a lot of time, money and ridicule for more than a century. He preached while he built and he didn't allow anyone to stop him, for God had spoken to him. Real faith is like this, it obeys, and it keeps obeying. Real faith sees things through to the end.

In all of this, in faith Noah put God first. We know this because the writer of Hebrews lets us know in verse 7: "By which he condemned the world and became heir of the righteousness which is according to faith." So Noah condemned the people of the world in the sense that his righteous life of faith exposed their unrighteous lives of unbelief. His righteousness aggravated their guilt. His life of obedient faith was like a bright light taken into a dark cavern. If it hadn't been for Noah, perhaps someone from that godless generation could have argued, "But I never knew how to live in a godly manner. I never heard about God's impending judgment." But Noah took away all their excuses. In faith, we are called to do the same to those around us. We are called to walk as children of the light, to expose the darkness, to stand up and stand out, and to show the world what true faith in the living God looks like. Only God knows how He will use your faithful life to impact this generation.

Think about it: we only have one opportunity here on this sinful planet, so we might as well burn as bright as we possibly can for Him. Judgment is coming for this world just as much as it was for those in

Noah's day. And just as the ark was the only means of salvation from God's judgment for Noah and his family, so the Lord Jesus Christ is the only way that God has provided for salvation from the judgment to come. Everyone on board the ark was saved and everyone not on the ark was lost. In like manner, everyone who has trusted in Christ as Lord and Savior will be saved, and everyone who has trusted in anything else will be lost. And here you are, and the door of the ark is still open. Please be faithful like Noah. Be fearful and obedient like he was, for who knows how God will use you to have an impact here for His glory?

CHAPTER 6

John Muir Trail:

One of the great incentives of hiking the John Muir Trail was getting to the end of the hike and standing on the top of Mount Whitney. Mount Whitney is the highest mountain in the contiguous United States and standing on top of it is incredibly rewarding. Looking out from its crest after completing our journey was even more rewarding. There's a sense of fulfillment with the completion of the trail, the completion of any hard task, really, but for me it's always been about reaching the end, finishing something that I've invested my heart and soul into. But no great accomplishment can be achieved without great adversity. Each day was becoming a huge struggle.

It was day four when the blisters showed up. Lots of them. I remember the day before when we came to a water crossing. The water was deep enough that everyone had to take off their boots and wade through the water. Sometimes at these creeks, there were rocks that you could use to hop across, and sometimes there might be a log or something to balance on and get across. But not here. As I was taking my hiking boots off there was a couple that had just cross the creek from the other side and were putting on their shows. They were quitting the hike after three days on the trail. Why? Because he had a blister "the size of a quarter" on the heel of his foot. Evidently the blister hurt enough to cause him to stop his JMT hike. The next day as I came down yet another pass, I decided it would be good to check my feet since they had begun to hurt. I stopped at a spot overlooking a beautiful lake with an incredible mountain peak behind it. I peeled my shoes and socks off and, not good. No wonder they hurt; five blisters on five different toes. Additionally, on one foot a nasty blister had formed on my heel. On the other, a big one stretched across the side of my foot. I taped them up and got my boots back on and then kept going. There wasn't anything else to do except hope they didn't get infected or start to hurt so badly that I'd want to quit.

At the same time that I was taking care of my feet, I had noticed how red the back of my shoulders appeared. It was from my backpack rubbing, but I shrugged it off. By the end of the next day the rubbing had grown painful, and that night in camp my back was a mass of nasty blisters where the straps of my backpack had taken their toll. They were painful to touch and looked extremely unpleasant. Because I couldn't reach them, Dave had to help by applying ointment to my back, placing gauze over the most serious of the blisters and then using duct tape to secure it all to my back. Dave wasn't happy about this! The tape stayed on for the rest of the hike. Because backpacks are designed to be worn a particular way, there was no chance of a reprieve from wearing it, so my torment grew as the days progressed, but it never hurt so bad that I wanted to quit. Peeling off the duct tape and the gauze from my shoulders and back at the end of the hike was quite the experience.

From that day on, I found myself wincing as blisters bit into my flesh with nearly every step. What had started as an occasional discomfort grew into a constant grimace that reflected my pain level. At times, I found myself asking why I felt the need to continue—it was painful out there and there had to be an easier way of going. Each day became worse with the exhaustive strain to pull and push myself up one side of a mountain only to endure the numbing sensations in my legs and feet as I plodded down the other side. By the end of each day everything hurt. And yet, I never felt pushed over the edge to where I wanted to stop and give up. In the midst of this, the goal to finish remained clear. I focused on achieving that goal—a goal that I saw transcend from my hike on a daily basis to my daily walk with the Lord. Finishing what I had started became a great motivation to keep going. How much more us in Christ?

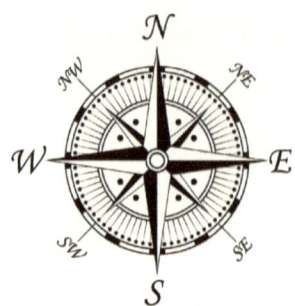

Faith Principle 7
Abraham: The faithful obey God (Part II)

We have seen how the faithful show forth their faith with loving action and obedience. We see that yet again in verses 8 through 12 in the example of Abraham.

> By faith Abraham obeyed when he was called to go out to the place which he would receive as an inheritance. And he went out, not knowing where he was going. By faith he dwelt in the land of promise as in a foreign country, dwelling in tents with Isaac and Jacob, the heirs with him of the same promise; for he waited for the city which has foundations, whose builder and maker is God. By faith Sarah herself also received strength to conceive seed, and she bore a child when she was past the age, because she judged Him faithful who had promised. Therefore from one man, and him as good as dead, were born as many as the stars of the sky in multitude—innumerable as the sand which is by the seashore.

We first hear about Abraham (Abram) at the end of Genesis 11. At that time, Abram lived in Ur of the Chaldeans, which is modern day Iraq. The city itself is no longer around, but its remains are located just south of Baghdad on the Euphrates River. Ur was a totally pagan city that was known to be a center for the worship of the false moon god, and Abram was a pagan himself who descended from a line of idolaters.

But then something incredible happened. God effectually called Abraham to Himself. God opened Abraham's blind spiritual eyes. God changed Abraham's heart of stone to a heart of flesh, and that's when Abraham believed and was saved. As Stephen said in Acts 7:2, "The God of glory appeared to our father Abraham when he was in Mesopotamia, before he dwelt in Haran." So God appeared to Abraham and he came to the Lord in saving faith, obeyed God by leaving Ur in Mesopotamia and he then settled in Haran for a few years until his father died. God then issued a call to Abraham in Genesis 12 to go to Canaan.

In Genesis 15:6, it says, "Abraham believed God, and it was accounted to Him as righteousness." This is talking about the saving faith that Abraham had before he left Ur at the end of Genesis 11. He believed before he obeyed, and he obeyed because he believed. This is important to understand so that we don't think that Abraham was somehow saved by his obedience or by some kind of work. No. Obedience always flows from true faith, but people are never saved because of their obedience, they are obedient because of their salvation.

So Abraham was saved and then he obeyed. The word *obeyed* used here literally means to listen with attentiveness, and to respond positively to what is heard.[40] This is what true faith does, it always obeys God. Yes, we are saved by faith alone and not by works, but saving faith is never alone. It results in obedience because love for God compels us to obey, for obedience proves that our faith truly is genuine faith.

Note that true faith in the Lord is heartfelt faith. It captures our hearts and fills us with love. It naturally overflows into action, and it is passionate. Jesus said, "If you love me, you will obey me." Of course. Can you imagine

---

[40] Kittel, 34.

hearing this: "I'm a wretched, dirty, rotten sinner and I deserve to go to hell because of my sin. On my own I'm doomed. But Jesus, out of His great, incredible love for me, died so I could live. He took all my sin onto Himself, and He was punished for it so that I could live and go to heaven. And now because of Him, I get heaven instead of hell, Him instead of Satan, grace instead of wrath, love instead of eternal judgment, joy instead of eternal gloom, and perfection and bliss instead of sin and eternal misery. But I'm not going to live like I believe it. I'm not going to live for His glory. I'm not going to obey Him."

What? Does that make any sense at all?

It certainly does not. For those who truly believe and are saved are overwhelmed with love back to Him. That love compels them to action, to obedience, to battling sin and to glorifying this God who gave us everything. In light of who He is and what He's done in saving your dead lost soul from wrath, do you not feel the love for Him from deep within? Are you not compelled to show that love with passionate obedience? Every Christian should feel this way. Abraham felt this way, and so, because of his faith, Abraham obeyed.

But that's not all. Notice that Abraham didn't even know where he was going. God said, "Abraham, go."

"Okay. Where, Lord?"

"That way."

"Okay, Lord. But where is the final destination?"

"Don't worry about that Abraham, just go and trust me."

"Okay, Lord, I'll go."

Amazing. And so, Abraham's obedient faith caused him to go "out to a place which he was to receive for an inheritance, and he went out, not knowing where he was going."

And consider this: God didn't tell him until later that the destination was Canaan, the Promised Land. Abraham had to leave his culture, his familiar way of life in Ur and later in Haran, his friends, his family and his earthly inheritance. It was a long and dangerous trip. But even so, Abraham obeyed, risking everything, based solely on God's promise.

You may look at this and say, "I wish I had a faith like that, a faith like Abel, Enoch, Noah and Abraham. But I'll never have perfect faith like them."

But who said they had perfect faith? We don't know much about Abel and Enoch. On the other hand, we know a bit more about Noah and Abraham. And the more we know, the more we see these people struggled just like we all struggle. They had lapses. The key is to be like them in their faith and unlike them in their lapses. The writer of Hebrews uses the positive examples of faith in these people to show us what it looks like and what it ought to look like more and more in our lives.

Later, we will look at Samson. Samson was a pretty wretched man. So how is he an example for us in faith? His example is seen at the end. Our call is to take that example at the end and use it in our own lives. It's simple, we take these good examples of faith and we apply them to our own lives, while the bad examples we leave behind. Look back at Noah. There's a good deal more to Noah's story and much of it was dreadful. After Noah got off the Ark and some time went by, Noah got drunk and naked, and shamed himself. Don't do that. Have faith like Noah in many ways, but don't be like Noah by getting drunk, naked and shaming yourself.

What about Abraham, the father of faith? Well, Stephen's speech in Acts 7 declares that God appeared to Abraham while he was living in Ur before he went to Haran. God said, "Get out of your country and from your relatives and go to the land I will show you."

Abraham obeyed. But wait, he took relatives with him, and Haran isn't in the Promised Land, it's north not west. And it wasn't until after Abraham's father died that God again appeared to him, and he fully obeyed.

But that's not all. After Abraham fully obeyed and traveled to Haran, we find in Genesis 12 that a famine was in the land. Because of this, Abraham left the Promised Land and sojourned in Egypt. There, he feared for his own life, even though God had made great promises to him, and those promises presumed that Abraham would live. But somehow Abraham feared that God wouldn't be able to protect him in Egypt, beyond the borders of the Promised Land. And so he instructed his wife Sarai to lie about her relationship to him. She was to say, "He's my brother," which was a half-truth but a full lie. In doing this, he put his wife in Pharaoh's harem. When the truth came out, even Pharaoh could see the wrong in this. By the way, a number of years later, virtually the same thing happened again.

On top of that, Genesis 16:1 says this:

> Now Sarai, Abram's wife, had not given birth to any children, but she had an Egyptian servant named Hagar. So Sarai said to Abram, "Since the Lord has prevented me from having children, have sexual relations with my servant. Perhaps I can have a family by her." Abram did what Sarai told him.

What? Really, Abraham? Even though God was clear that the promised child would come through Sarah, not her servant. Where's the faith? Obviously, he let fear overcome him, and he didn't act in faith here at all. So why is he mentioned as an example of faith in Hebrews 11 with all these marks against him?

Well, who else is the writer going to use as examples for us but sinful and fallible people? Even the best of men are men at best. And these lapses don't change the fact that we can learn much from Abraham's faith. And so, we take the good and learn from it and let it inspire us. And then we throw out the bad and we learn from that as well. Both Noah and

Abraham were saved men who loved the Lord and who sought to live for His glory. But they weren't perfect, and neither are we. They messed up at times, but their direction was clear, and we can learn from them today. When you fall and fail, in faith get back at it right away and keep going. Always remember that our God is a gracious and forgiving God.

Abraham obeyed even though he didn't know where he was going. We too don't know what the near future will hold. What's the story with my health? What about my finances? What about my job? Something else? No matter, I trust the Lord. For He is someone we can trust even when we don't know exactly what lies ahead in the immediate future. That said, we do know the ultimate end, and it's all good for us in Christ. Until then, stay faithful and obey.

Faith Principle 8
The faithful look ahead

The writer of Hebrews continues by telling us "Abraham lived in tents." I've done a number of backpacking trips and have learned something about living in tents: it's fun for about a day. After that it gets extremely mundane, especially when you have to pack it up and take it to another place. Verse 9 continues, "By faith he dwelt in the land of promise as in a foreign country, dwelling in tents with Isaac and Jacob, the heirs with him of the same promise." Isn't this interesting? Abraham, the heir to the Promised Land, never owned a foot of ground in it, except for the Cave of Machpelah, which he bought at full cost to bury his wife.

Where was the inheritance that Abraham had expected? It lay ahead. Without real faith in the God who saved him, he might have even thought that he had been deceived by God. But Abraham didn't waiver, and even though he had lapses as a sinful human being, he continued to trust God through it all.

This speaks to us today. As the faithful who love the Lord, we often have to live in this world with conditions that seemingly contradict the promises of God. Sometimes God's people face tribulation. They encounter distress, persecution, famine and nakedness. Some will face peril; some will deal with cancer and even death. Each of us will endure heartache and tragedy. Our faith in God and what He has promised is what will pull us through. He knows. He is good. He has me and He promises to work all this out. I trust Him. The faithful trust Him even when things seem bleak.

Like Abraham, we are pilgrims in a foreign land, and we don't really belong here. We need to adopt the mindset of pilgrims. When we travel in a foreign country, we stand out as different. The locals can spot us. They know that we are not one of them. Yes, we may temporarily adopt some of their local customs, but on most things, it's evident that we think and live differently, according to the customs of our homeland.

As Christians, our homeland is heaven. We are different than the locals here. Our mindset is different, our language is different, our purpose is different, everything is different. What does it matter if we're living in tents when we know something better awaits us? The hopes of the natives of this earthly land center on this life only. They try to accumulate all things and engage in all activities, which they believe will bring them happiness in this life only. But our hopes center in Jesus Christ and on our eternal inheritance in Him. And so we hold the things of this life loosely. Yes, we enjoy all that God provides, but we know that our real treasures are in heaven and that's what compels us in this fading life. Although Abraham never fit in because of his allegiance to God, he was, as Kent Hughes put it, "A happy camper."[41] Literally. Why? Because in faith he looked ahead.

---

[41] Hughes, 326.

Verse 10 says Abraham "waited for the city which has foundations, whose builder and maker is God." This is wonderful. The city with foundations stands in contrast with life in a tent, which has no foundation. And since God is both the architect and builder of this city, the foundations are solid and secure, unlike any earthly city today that can be taken down through fire, flood or earthquake. But not this city of God. And while in most cities today the people want to get out and move to the suburbs, this city that God has designed and built is one that we all want to reside in.

What is this city? The city Abraham waited for is the eternal city that God has prepared for His people, the city of the living God. The writer calls it the "heavenly country," in verse 16, and then in 12:22 refers to it as the "heavenly Jerusalem." Abraham lived for this; his heart belonged to the city to come, and he placed his hopes there by faith in the Lord. In faith, he had an eternal perspective, and he was willing to forsake the present comforts for the future glory that belonged to him as a child of God. He fixed his eyes on the city ahead. He was like the character, Christian, in the book *Pilgrim's Progress* who was beaten down by the journey he had to walk in his Christian life.[42] He faced one hardship after another, one trial after another, one struggle after another and he was worn out by the battle. But then after a long climb up a mountain, he caught a glimpse of his destination—the celestial city, the heavenly city, the city with foundations whose builder and architect is God. That glimpse gave him strength to keep going to the end. And while he still had many trials, dangers, fears and struggles, he always remembered the city that was waiting for him, where God Himself was waiting for Him. And

---

[42] John Bunyan, *Pilgrims Progress in Modern English*, (Chicago, IL: Moody Publishers, 1992), 54.

so, he continued on. That was Abraham. And that should be us as well. In faith we look ahead.

Think of what we have waiting for us in Christ. The revered 19th century minister Edward Dorr Griffin obviously did. The first pastor of Boston's historic Park Street Church in 1811, and as the president of Williams College from 1821 to 1836, Griffin had a few things to say about this heavenly city. His thoughts were presented to his congregation in a sermon entitled, "Heaven."

> Heaven is a world of more resplendent and varied beauty than mortal eye has ever seen. There—the saints are forever delivered from the interruptions of the wicked, from the pollution of their society, and from the disgusting coarseness of their conversation—and we are admitted to the most intimate friendship with the holy angels, with patriarchs, prophets, apostles, martyrs, and the whole assembly that have been collecting since the death of Abel, including, in many instances, the most beloved friends they knew on earth. Parents will there meet with their children, and husbands their wives, after a long and painful separation. Brothers and sisters will rush into each other's arms and exclaim, "Have I found you at last? This is far unlike the parting hour when I closed your eyes, and far unlike the solitary evenings in which I have visited your grave and wept over your dust." Those blessed spirits will enjoy the most perfect friendship, with every distrust and rival interest banished; each loving the other as his own soul and filled with joy unspeakable.

How exciting. Griffin continued:

> All the glory and happiness there will be eternal. If to know and love God in one degree makes a heaven, to know and love him in ten degrees will make a tenfold happiness. The time must come when the feeblest saint in heaven will enjoy more in one hour than all the creations of God have enjoyed to this day; and still he has just begun his eternal progress in blessedness.[43]

What a great description, and that's just a glimpse. And it's coming for us in Christ. How can we not be excited about this? How can we not run towards this with more fervor? How can this not stir us up to greater faith, and greater action and obedience until we arrive? The trials many face here are not trivial—poor health, loss of a job and the rejection by the culture are difficult. It's only when we consider eternity that we can deal with these disappointments in hope. This world isn't your real home. Think of how the world will appear to you a million ages after the judgment. What will you think as you're lost among the glories of heaven? The call? To faithfully live for what lies ahead.

Oh yes, Abraham had some trials on his road of faith. But overall, he's a great example for us, and he tells us to obey even when you don't understand and to patiently endure knowing that something much greater lies ahead. This is what the faithful do.

---

[43] Edward Griffin, "Heaven," Grace Gems, accessed on 1/25/2021, https://gracegems.org/B/Griffin_heaven.htm

CHAPTER 7

John Muir Trail:

There were many reasons why I wanted to complete the John Muir Trail, but two of those reasons stand out above the others. First, was standing on top of Mount Whitney at the end of the trail. I had been to the summit of Whitney before, from the other direction to the west. But I'd never reached it from the back side of the mountain from the east. I was eagerly looking forward to standing on the top of the peak, having just completed a grueling trail and celebrating a hard accomplishment with my friend. I knew it would be very rewarding.

Second, I couldn't wait to reward myself with the hamburger, fries and coke that awaited me at the Whitney Portal. We knew that the people there served some very good food at the portal, where the trail ended. Note that while the trail ends on the top of Mount Whitney, you have to hike eleven more miles down the Mount Whitney trail to the Whitney Portal, where you can get picked up. I read in a book that the Whitney Portal store not only serves great hamburgers, but that they also serve incredible breakfasts, including pancakes as big as car tires. Dave and I couldn't wait to get off the trail and gorge ourselves on the food that awaited us. It was great incentive. Finishing a hard task with a friend and devouring some great food after surviving on oatmeal and Clif Bars for two weeks was something we eagerly looked forward to. Good food is one thing, but just think about all the incentives we have in Christ to finish strong.

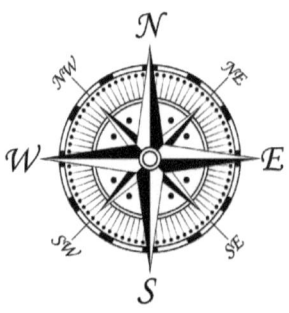

Faith Principle 9
Sarah: The faithful embrace God's promises

Sarah is the next example of faith for us to follow. Hebrews 11:11-12:

> By faith Sarah herself also received strength to conceive seed, and she bore a child when she was past the age, because she judged Him faithful who had promised. Therefore from one man, and him as good as dead, were born as many as the stars of the sky in multitude—innumerable as the sand which is by the seashore.

So, in faith Sarah received strength to conceive. The call? Have faith like Sarah. If you remember, Abraham and Sarah were unable to conceive children. Even so, God promised them not only a son, but also nations of descendants. To highlight the promise, God changed his name from

Abram, which means high father, to Abraham which means father of a multitude, even though he was childless.[44] From Genesis 17:5-6, God said, "I will make you exceedingly fruitful, and I will make nations of you, and kings will come forth from you." But again, not only were Abraham and Sarah unable to conceive children, but they were also both really old; way too old to have children.

The first part of verse 11 is interesting because it's not clear in the original who the real subject is, Sarah or Abraham. That phrase *received strength to conceive seed* literally means "power for the laying down of seed," which changes things a bit.[45] So without getting too technical, the first part of this verse is probably referring to Abraham's faith more than Sarah's. The sense is this: By faith, even though Sarah was barren, he, Abraham, received power to beget. This shows his trust in God to give him a child.

You might remember that in Genesis 18, Sarah was rebuked for her unbelief regarding this. She laughed when she heard she would have a son, and when the Lord confronted her, she denied rather than confessed her unbelief. That said, the second part of this verse makes it clear that Sarah eventually came to believe God's promise as Abraham did. But here in the first part of this verse, it seems that the main focus is on the faith of Abraham. God said it, he believed it and he trusted God. Sarah was 90 when she had Isaac, and then on top of that, God's promise to Abraham happened 24 years earlier. That's a long time to wait, but true faith waits and trusts.

Too many people these days have a very short-sighted faith. They trust God, but when things don't happen according to their desires, their faith

---

[44] Hughes, 247.
[45] Kenneth Wuest, *Wuest's Word Studies from the Greek New Testament: for the English reader*, vol. 10, (Grand Rapids, MI: Eerdmans, 1997), 202.

weakens. That's not the faith that God commends. The faith that God commends is a continuing faith, an enduring faith, and a faith that trusts God all the way to the very end.

Note that this doesn't mean that everyone who is having trouble conceiving a child will be able to conceive a child if they just had enough faith. Abraham and Sarah had a clear promise from God, but that's not a promise for everyone. So, what do we do? We pray, we trust God and we pray some more. If things don't turn out the way we expect or want them to turn out, we trust Him with that, knowing that He knows what He's doing with us. Real faith trusts God even when things don't turn out the way we have planned. This earth is full of trials, disappointments and hurts, but not so in our heavenly city. We look to that, and in faith we let that vision move us forward. This world is not our real home.

In the second part of verse 11, we are now clearly looking at Sarah. "She judged Him faithful." In other words, she trusted God, the God who is faithful in all His ways, the God who keeps all His promises. So, you progress from Abraham to both Abraham and Sarah, and now to Sarah. Sarah does indeed have true faith in the living God. She judged Him faithful. That word *judge* means to consider, to think, to regard and to reckon. [46] In other words, she trusted Him because she knew the faithfulness of God. She grew in her faith, and she knew firsthand that God keeps His promises—not always in the time we like, but always nonetheless, and she trusted Him with that.

The word for *faithful* means reliable, trustworthy and dependable.[47] The opposite of being faithful is to be changing and unstable. God is never unstable. He is always faithful. His word is always faithful. God speaks never-ending truth, and the promises He made to them still hold true

---

[46] Brown, vol. 2, 822.
[47] Louw, vol. 1, 376.

because He doesn't change. That was an anchor for them, and also for us in Christ today. For if God said it, He will certainly do it. Our God is immutable, He's unchanging, and that means that He is completely trustworthy in everything. And this trustworthy God has made many promises to you His beloved child, not necessarily having a child in old age, but many amazing promises nonetheless, and you are called to trust Him even when those promises don't seem to be possible for you.

Here are just a few of the promises that God has made, starting in the Old Testament. And note that these OT promises have application for us in Him today. God promised that if we truly search for Him, we will find Him. God promised protection for His children. God promised that His love will never fail. God promised Israel that their sin could be forgiven, and their nation healed when they repent and seek Him. This most definitely applies to us today. God promised blessing for all who will delight themselves in His Word.

In the New Testament, God promised salvation to all who believe in His Son. God promised that all things will work out for good for His children. God promised comfort in our trials. God promised new life and every spiritual blessing in Christ, and that our eternal inheritance is reserved for us. God promised to finish the work He started in us. God promised peace when we pray. God promised to supply our true needs. Jesus promised rest, abundant life and eternal life to those who trust Him. Jesus also promised to hold us securely, saying, "No one will snatch them out of my hand." Jesus promised that He will return for us. These promises go on and on. So many incredible promises, and they are sure and solid promises. And God is faithful to keep all His promises to us.

Sarah judged Him faithful who had promised, and so can you. She grew in her faith, and she knew the child was coming—an amazing miracle. Think about it, a 90-year-old giving birth. Faith is trusting in the character of God before we see how He is going to work things out. As a child trusts a loving father, we can trust our heavenly Father to always do what is right even when it seems wrong to us. For faith sees beyond the fading things of this short life. As A.W. Tozer said:

> True faith rests upon the character of God and asks no further proof than the moral perfections of the One who cannot lie. It is enough that God said it, and if the statement should contradict every one of the five senses and all the conclusions of logic as well, still the believer continues to believe. "Let God be true, but every man a liar" is the language of true faith.[48]

That's right. So, I trust Him more than I trust anyone or anything else. And the reason is because He's perfectly trustworthy.

Look at verse 12: "Therefore from one man, and him as good as dead, were born as many as the stars of the sky in multitude—innumerable as the sand which is by the seashore."

Think about that. Abraham was as good as dead, and this still happened. And note that the promises of God for Abraham weren't seen by him in this life. Yet he still trusted God. What really did Abraham get in this life for his life of faith and obedience? Well, he was uprooted from family and friends, never to see them again. He had nowhere to call home other than tents, moving from place to place, and in the end, just one sole legitimate child. Yes, he lived to see Isaac, the son of the promise born, and he even lived 15 years after the birth of Jacob, but he didn't see any of Jacob's sons. He didn't live long enough to get even a hint of the fulfillment of God's promise to multiply his descendants as the stars or the sand. As 11:13 says, he really did "die in faith, without receiving the

---

[48] A.W. Tozer, *Man: The Dwelling Place of God*, accessed 2/3/2020, https://www.worldinvisible.com/library/tozer/5j00.0010/5j00.0010.07.htm

promises." From Abraham's perspective, even though he lived for 175 years, God's promises weren't fulfilled. He died with one son and two grandsons, hardly an innumerable nation.

But God's promises did not fail in any way. From Abraham's offspring came the people of Israel. Even more, from God's timeframe, the true children of Abraham—those who believe in Abraham's seed, Jesus Christ—they number in the billions. God has a way of doing way more than we could ever think or imagine. Our call: trust Him. We see dimly but faith looks ahead, and the future is bright for us in Christ. Trust Him no matter what, for God is always faithful.

CHAPTER 8

American River 50-mile Run:

Oh no. I felt the sharp sting in my knee with about ten miles left in my 50-mile ultra-marathon. I'd just stepped off the trail to let another runner pass (something, I admit, I was used to doing), but as I merged back onto the trail, I landed wrong on my foot and a spasm shot up through my knee. My first thought was simple enough: this was not good. Immediately, I pictured myself slowing to a walk and hobbling off to the side of the trail. I wouldn't be able to finish, which was a hard pill for me to swallow, especially after having come so far. On top of that, I hate quitting. I despise it. I could see all of this in the picture I was constructing in my head. I pulled up and hopped the last couple of steps as I moved off the trail. I actually wanted to cry.

This ultra-marathon had a time cap of fourteen hours, and I was about ten hours in. I told myself I might as well keep moving forward until the fourteen hours were up. After a few cautious steps to gauge the level of pain, I found I could walk even if I couldn't run. So I walked, gingerly at first. After a short distance I found I could add a little pace. Amazingly, just a short distance from where I'd tweaked my knee, I was finding the pain level bearable, it hurt but it wasn't the knee-buckling agony I'd feared I'd suffered. I started to move with purpose. Soon I was able to run. Slowly. But that's how I run anyhow.

If you were to look at me, there's little chance you would mistake me for one of those ultra-runner types. To put it nicely, I do not have a runner's lean frame, let alone the ultra-runner's super-athlete shape. But I enjoy running and I like challenges, and so it was in October that I signed up for the American River 50 Mile Endurance Run in April. This is the second largest 50 miler in the United States, with a course that begins in Folsom and traverses the Sierra Nevada foothills through oak woodlands and meadows, across bridges and creeks, and along spectacular trails all the way to Auburn. My goal wasn't to capture one of the top finishing positions or to set some personal time goal for the run. No, I'm more realistic than that; I wanted to finish under the 14-hour time cap. There was a reward at the end of the race for runners I was looking forward to as well.

Preparing for the run proved brutal. For months, anyone training for such a race not only has to run numerous times throughout the week, but has to do a long run every week, with each week adding more miles. Once my long runs reached over fifteen miles, it began messing with my head. As I started each of my long runs, I would think to myself, "I have to do this for three more hours and I am already tired!" Not good. But I persisted. I mean, what else was I going to do? I had already paid the entry fee for the run.

No, I told myself, there's no way that I was not going to at least show up and do my best.

Eventually, race day came. I was up at 4:30 a.m. and drove an hour from home to where the race started. I was at the starting point early and waited in my car for a half hour until race time. I felt a little jittery with excitement, yet at the same time I was nervous. I tried to think of other things to keep my mind occupied. I thought of the special reward that runners would receive at the finish line. It wasn't working, I kept coming back to wondering how would I do? Would I be able to finish under the time? Would I be able to finish it all? Was I prepared enough? I was about to find out. For this race, runners left in waves, and when it was time, the group I was a part of lined up and focused as the countdown began. I glanced around and realized everyone else looked like a runner except for me. Again, not good. I caught the last of the count: three, two, one . . . and we were off.

The first half of the race actually went pretty well. My last training run had been a 31 miler that I was able to finish and felt pretty good about, so I was confident that I could do at least a marathon. For the initial miles, the course remained fairly flat and paved, and by the time I arrived at mile-marker 25, I was certainly tired, but felt pretty good. Unfortunately, that changed quickly.

The best part about arriving at the halfway mark was that my daughter, Katie, was able to run the rest of the race with me. She helped me way more than you could ever think. The second half of the race is not easy. It is a single-track dirt trail that runs through the foothills and is not flat in any way. Runners are either going up or going down. The stress from the hills affected me immediately, but my daughter helped. "Keep going, Dad," she'd call out as we ran, sometimes side-by-side but more often in single file. "You're doing good. Don't quit! The next aid station is up ahead." Five miles later I was tanked. There were still twenty more miles to go.

My wife, Tiffany, waited for me at one of the aid stations. She had a folding chair set up for me with some food and a Coke. I pulled in and plopped down, utterly beat. Tiff later told me how shocked she was when she saw me at that aid station; that I looked like a dead man walking. She thought there was no way I would finish. However, the energy boost from the food and soda she had waiting for me, plus the encouragement from my daughter gave me some renewed energy.

Katie and I took off slowly, hoping to make it to the next aid station. We walked the hills from there on out, and we shuffled along at a slow pace when the trail flattened out, or on rare occasions when we were going downhill. It was pretty slow going, but we never stopped, and Katie kept encouraging me along. Every time we came to a flat stretch on the trail, or the trail went downhill, Katie would say, "Go." And I went, even though I wanted to continue walking. There came a point where I probably would have quit if she wasn't there with me. I didn't quit because I hate quitting, but also, I didn't quit because I didn't want to let Katie down. She was working so hard to encourage me to keep going. Because of her I kept going.

The next couple of aid stations were wonderful, as the volunteers encouraged and helped with food and water. Katie continued to encourage and challenge me, and eventually, we crossed the finish line side-by-side. I wouldn't have wanted it any other way, with an hour and a half to spare from missing the cutoff. It was a great feeling to finish something that was so hard. Tiff and our other two daughters were waiting at the finish line, and I could tell they were proud of my accomplishment. I made my way over with other runners to accept our reward, a chicken chipotle burrito that tasted marvelous. And on the way home, we stopped and enjoyed frozen yogurt—all of us as a family celebration.

Lesson: keep going, never quit. Have other people around you who can encourage you on the journey. Get good nourishment along the way. Look to the reward at the end and continue on.

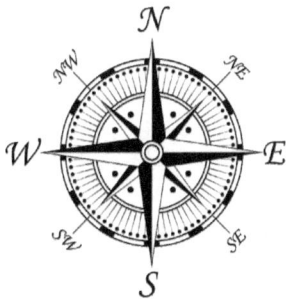

Faith Principle 10
The Patriarchs: The faithful die trusting God

Remember, Hebrews 11 looks at the lives of the faithful, and it uses those faithful ones as examples to spur us on in our own faith. The call: have faith like them. They weren't perfect but they were faithful, they pressed on, they obeyed, they got up and continued on when they fell. In those areas they are great examples for us.

The writer has just finished speaking about Abraham when he writes these words in Hebrews 11:13-16:

> These all died in faith, not having received the promises, but having seen them afar off were assured of them, embraced them

> and confessed that they were strangers and pilgrims on the earth. For those who say such things declare plainly that they seek a homeland. And truly if they had called to mind that country from which they had come out, they would have had opportunity to return. But now they desire a better, that is, a heavenly country. Therefore God is not ashamed to be called their God, for He has prepared a city for them.

What an inspiring passage. Verse 13 starts out, "These all died in faith." So, the question is who are "these all?" Some commentaries say that this refers to everyone that he's mentioned so far in Hebrews 11. But that's not true because not everyone died in Hebrews 11. Enoch didn't die. Because of that, most believe that the "these all" is referring to the patriarchs of the faith, namely, Abraham, Isaac and Jacob. On top of that, the promises that are mentioned in verse 13, specifically the promises of land and innumerable offspring, began with Abraham and were then passed down to Isaac and then to Jacob. So it seems that this is specifically talking about the patriarchs of the faith—the fathers of the faith: Abraham, Isaac and Jacob.[49]

They died in faith, which is the best way to die—in faith and full of trust in the Lord. Death is the final test of faith, and these patriarchs all passed the test with flying colors, living by faith right up to the last breath. And look, they died in faith though never receiving the fullness of the universal blessing that had been promised to them. But even so, they still believed. They still clung to the Lord in faith. They still trusted.

Think about that. For most of us, there might be some discontent with God when, after years and years in a foreign land, none of His

---

[49] Richard Philips, *Hebrews: Reformed Expository Commentary*, (Phillipsburg, New Jersey: P&R Publishing:, 2006), 458.

promises came true in our lifetimes. Abraham left his home, and he even witnessed the death of his wife in this foreign land. But that didn't weaken his faith. Instead, he accepted his circumstance and he continued to trust the Lord.

Note that *in faith* literally reads "according to faith."[50] In other words, they died "in keeping with their life of faith." So they died, as they lived. They died dominated by faith. Their faith didn't waiver on their death bed, but it remained and even grew stronger. And so, they trusted Him until they came to their graves. God isn't the God of apostates who turn back. He's the God of those who trust Him in life and in death, faithful to the end. For us in Christ, the best is ahead of us, and the majority of God's promises lie on the other side of our final earthly breath. Spurgeon said it like this:

> The faith that many waters cannot drown and the fiercest fires cannot burn—the faith that plods on throughout a long and weary life—the faith that labors on, doing whatever service God appoints it—the faith that waits patiently, expecting the time when every promise of God shall be fulfilled to the letter when its hour has come—that is the faith which makes him such a man that God is not ashamed to be called his God.[51]

I think of the Apostle Paul near the end of his life, writing to Timothy in 2 Timothy 4:6-8, when he says, "I have fought the fight, I have finished the race, I have kept the faith, and now the crown awaits." The call is to be like that. To continue on, to finish well, to finish strong and to run the

---

[50] Hughes, 477.
[51] Charles Spurgeon, "The Two Pivots", accessed 4/5/2020, https://www.spurgeongems.org/sermon/chs2633.pdf

race faithfully every day because who knows when our last day will come? The crown awaits.

Why should Christians not fear death? Because we know what lies ahead, the promises of God, like the patriarchs knew in faith. Their promises weren't realized in this life, but they knew they would come true because God made those promises to them. In the book *Pilgrim's Progress*, Christian and Hopeful are at the end of their lives. They have battled and they have struggled through their journey, and they have overcome. They continued on in faith to the end, and now the celestial city is in sight. It's right there, the city made with foundations formed and built by God. Both men understand that heaven and eternal glory are right there in front of them. But to get there they must cross the river Jordan—the river of death. It's the final challenge that stands between them and being face to face with their Lord.[52] They look for a bridge, but they can find nothing.

They ask, "Is there any other way to the gate of the city?"

They learn there is another way, but they're told only Enoch and Elijah have reached the gate without crossing the river and without dying. Christian and Hopeful must cross the river.

As they prepare to wade into the water, they are told, "You will find the river deeper or shallower according to your faith in the Lord."

Hopeful moves through the river of death in full stride, full of faith. Next to him, Christian has a harder time of it, and he struggles not only with the pull of the water but with the knowledge of his death.

Hopeful calls, "Be of good cheer my brother, for I feel the bottom and it is firm."

Even so, Christian's faith begins to wane, and so he struggles with his final earthly trial of death. He fears he will be lost before he can reach the city. Hopeful continues to encourage him, gives him scripture and

---

[52] Bunyan, 151.

reminds him of the goodness of God. Hopeful calls out to his friend Christian, even when all seems lost. He directs him towards the savior, and it's after that, Christian then discovers solid ground in which to wade across the river and reach the gate of the city of God.[53]

We are all going to have to cross that river, death, and the prayer is that we will walk right up to it, knowing the gate of the heavenly city is on the other side, and we dive on in, full of faith. When John Bunyan, the author of *Pilgrim's Progress*, was on his death bed and faced his own crossing of that river, he told those around him, "Weep not for me, but weep for yourselves. For I go to the Father, while you remain here."[54] I want to die like that. Full of faith, and ready to see Him. Like the patriarchs.

Faith Principle 11
The faithful embrace the promises of God

Next, we find that the patriarchs believed and embraced the promises. Having seen them afar off, they were assured of them, and they embraced them. This is interesting because verse 17 says that Abraham "had received the promises." So, in what sense did he not receive the promises, as verse 13 states? In the sense that the patriarchs didn't receive the total fulfillment of God's promises in this life. They only received a taste of them. Abraham and Sarah finally received the promise of a son in Isaac. But if you remember, Abraham died with only two heirs according to the promise, Isaac and Jacob, hardly an innumerable nation. Isaac owned a few wells, plus some grazing land for his flocks. But he still lived in a tent, and he wasn't in any significant way the heir of the land. Jacob died with about 70 descendants, including his sons who became the leaders of the

---

[53] Ibid, 155.
[54] David B. Calhoun, *In Their Own Words*, (Edinburgh: Banner of Truth Trust, 2018), 228.

12 tribes of Israel. But they were forced to move out of the land into Egypt where they then became slaves. You see, the patriarchs had a taste of the fulfillment of the promises, but it was only a taste. They saw them from a distance, but they weren't fully realized during their life. Still, they were assured of them, and in faith they embraced those promises.

The word *embraced* is interesting. It means to greet, to welcome and to salute.[55] The picture is of people on a ship passing a land that they can see on the horizon, waving a greeting to that land. They see it, they know it's there and they welcome it warmly. That's the picture of how the patriarchs treated the promises of God. Soon the greeting will turn into an embrace, but not yet. And that's okay because they know it is only a matter of time before they will embrace them. The same is true with us in Christ today. Heaven is on the horizon for us who believe; the full promises of God lie ahead. So right now, we look ahead in faith, eagerly, expectantly, waving until we get to embrace and finally reach the land where all the promises of God will be fulfilled. There, the eternal inheritance that is incorruptible, undefiled and unfading will be ours. Glory in all its fullness, where we will be in His presence and joy unspeakable will be forever ours. We wave to it now, but in faith we know that we will soon embrace it. For we trust, we have that confidence, that assurance, that eager expectation because the God who doesn't lie told us about it and has promised it to us.

The faith of the patriarchs can encourage us today, for soon we will indeed walk by sight. Until then, welcome the promises of God as friends that you will very soon embrace. Right now, we are still at a distance from them but soon we will reach land. The faithful understand this and they live like they believe it.

---

[55] Liddell, 124.

Faith Principle 12
The faithful live like strangers and pilgrims on the earth

Notice that the patriarchs confessed they were strangers and pilgrims on the earth. The word *confessed* means to say the same thing as another, to agree and to acknowledge a fact publicly.[56] Here we see that the patriarchs were fully aware that they didn't really belong on this earth. They even spoke about that fact; they clearly acknowledged that obvious truth.

"I'm a stranger and pilgrim here," they might say. And it seems that everyone around them knew it. Note that while that was true of them in a physical sense, for they were indeed living as pilgrims in tents in a foreign land, it was even more true for them in a spiritual sense, and that's what verse 13 is clearly talking about. For what was true for them physically, was also true for them spiritually. It's true for us spiritually as well. For we are strangers here, exiled for a time from our homeland.

The word *stranger* means a foreigner.[57] In the ancient world, the fate of a stranger was hard. A stranger was regarded with hatred, suspicion and contempt. In fact, being poor was considered better than living as a stranger in a foreign country. But even so, every believer is a stranger, a foreigner, an exile here on planet Earth, for this isn't our real home. As William Barclay said, "It was not that the Christians were foolishly otherworldly, detaching themselves from the life and work of this world; but they always remembered that they were people on the way."[58] They were only passing through, short-timers. Puritan writer Thomas Manton said this about strangers:

---

[56] Kittel, 687.
[57] Liddell, 539.
[58] William Barclay, Hebrews, accessed on 4/3/2020, https://www.studylight.org/commentaries/eng/dsb/hebrews-11.html

1) A stranger is one that is absent from his country, and from his father's house... so are we—for heaven is our country, God is there, and Christ is there. 2) A stranger in a foreign country is not known, nor valued according to his birth and breeding so the saints walk up and down in the world like princes in disguise. 3) Strangers are liable subject to inconveniences... so are godly men and women in the world... 4) A stranger is patient and is contented with pilgrim's fare and lodging. We are now abroad and must expect hardship. 5) A stranger is thankful for the least favor; so we must be thankfully contented with the things God hath bestowed upon us: anything in a strange country is much. 6) A stranger, that has a journey to go on, would pass over it as soon as he could, and so we, who have a journey to heaven, desire to finally get there. 7) A stranger buys not such things as he cannot carry with him. In like manner, our greatest care should be to gather those things that will abide with us in glory. 8) A stranger's heart is in his country; so is a saint's—in heaven. 9) A stranger provides for his return, as a merchant, that he may return richly laden. So we must appear before God in glory. Let us return from our travel well provided.[59]

He's right. Are you living like a stranger here, or have you put down roots as if this was your real and only true home? In faith, the patriarchs knew that they were strangers in Canaan, but also in this world. They lived like they believed it. In faith, we in Christ agree with Abraham, Isaac and Jacob; that this world isn't our true home. Our time here is brief and temporary and we're eagerly looking for our permanent home, the city of

---

[59] Charles Spurgeon, *The Treasury of David*, vol. 1, (Peabody, MA: Hendrickson Publishers), 230-231.

God in heaven. And in faith we live like it. For we are journeying by faith from an old city that is cursed and under threat of judgment to a blessed and heavenly city where our Lord dwells. We in Christ are registered citizens of heaven; our names are there, our Father is there, our Savior is there, our home is there, our fellow saints are there, and our inheritance is there. We need to live like we believe it. Faith will allow us to do that. Physically, for most of us, our citizenship is here in America, but the reality is that we in Christ are citizens of heaven. Heaven is our true home. So why then would we try to live like this earth is our home? Moving day is just around the corner, and who knows when our moving day will come?

Here's a question: does your conduct give you away as a citizen of heaven? Is it clear that you are a stranger and pilgrim on this sinful planet? It should be, not because we're so odd but because we are like Christ. Because in faith we live differently. Because we have different values. Because we aren't so worldly minded—no, we love, we forgive and we serve. We honor God when it's hard, and we have joy and peace that passes understanding. We have an eternal perspective, and don't despair and lose hope in trials and tragedies. We fight sin and pursue holiness, and we have morals that honor the Lord. We live so as to please our God in heaven, not ourselves.

This sinful planet isn't our real home. Aren't you glad? If this was all there was, we might as well throw up our hands in despair. It's a good thing this isn't our real home. Faith allows us to live like we believe it.

A few more watches keeping
A few more foes to down
As pilgrims brave we journey
To win the victor's crown![60]

Faith Principle 13
The faithful seek a homeland

The next truth that we see about the patriarchs is that they sought a homeland. Verse 14 states, "For those who say such things declare plainly that they seek a homeland." *Declare plainly* means to emphasize, to make clear, to make public and to make it plain.[61] Here we see that the patriarchs were keenly aware of the fact that they were strangers and pilgrims, and so they earnestly sought to please God as citizens of heaven. *Homeland* means hometown, a fatherland, the place where our father dwells, which is talking about the heavenly country where our heavenly father resides. In faith, that's not only what God's people seek, but we can't help but declare it plainly to the people around us because we're so excited to get there. *Seek* means to crave, to wish for, to desire and to have an intense longing for.[62]

What they longed for was home. I think the people around Abraham, Isaac and Jacob heard about their true home all the time. And again, not Ur, not their earthly hometown, but their true homeland, the city of God, the heavenly country. These patriarchs were consumed with it. They were like Dorothy in the Wizard of Oz. She longed to return to what she loved. "There's no place like home," she would repeat. "There's no place like

---

[60] "Hebrews", Precept Austin, accessed 5/3/2020, https://www.preceptaustin.org/hebrews_11_sermon_illustrations
[61] Kittel, 1244.
[62] Louw, 331.

home, there's no place like home." For the patriarchs, there was no place like home.

I would ask, "How do you know? You've never been there?"

If we could hear one of them speak, their answer would be simple and full of truth. "My heart is there," they would say. "My God is there, my true home is there, my affections are there, and soon I'll be there too—home."

If you long for something, if you love something, if you are excited about something, then you will talk about it to others. That's why the patriarchs declared plainly to others the thing that was foremost on their hearts; home, the place where their beloved Lord resides. It was this love that compelled them forward, always forward. In faith, they never wearily gave up the journey. Instead, they lived in hope, and they died in expectation. And they talked about it constantly.

So why are so many Christians today so silent? So ashamed? So lethargic? Because we've lost sight of home. We've become too worldly minded; our faith is wavering. How sad. Especially when this world has nothing to offer but sadness, misery, crushed hopes and dreams, and death. This world certainly has nothing lasting to offer.

So why set your affections on things that fade and rot when you could be loving and pleasing the God of eternity? Sadly, we are way too frivolous with the things of eternity. We waste our lives away on foolish things when we could be pleasing the Lord. We talk to people about the big game when we could be telling them about heaven and how to get there. We watch television when we should be praying and drawing nearer to our beloved Lord. We focus too much on self, as we push God off to the side. How foolish and short sighted.

We need to have the vision of the patriarchs, or of Paul, who basically said in Philippians 3:7,14, "Everything is a loss compared to Christ my all in all. Compared to Him everything else is dung, so there's one thing I do;

I press on in Him until I make it home." This is what consumes the faithful men and women of God who aren't sidetracked by sin and by the world.

Faith Principle 14
The faithful desire a heavenly country

The next truth about the patriarchs is that they desired a heavenly country. In verse 15, we read, "And truly if they had called to mind that country from which they had come out, they would have had an opportunity to return. But now they desire a better, that is, a heavenly country." What does this mean?

Remember, in Hebrews, the author is writing to people who were encountering hardships in their new lives as Christians. They were even tempted to go back to their old religion. So here, the writer points out that the patriarchs could have returned to Mesopotamia, to Ur, if they had been looking for an earthly inheritance. The living conditions in their former earthly homeland were probably far more developed than in the land of Canaan. If they had returned their family and friends would have welcomed them with open arms. While in Canaan, they were kept at a distance, so they could have returned. But if they did, they would have been disobeying the Lord, and so they didn't go back. Instead, they endured the hardships and in faith, they chose to obey God. They lived in tents because they were seeking a better country, that is, a heavenly one. For in faith, they knew that suffering and obeying God was better than living in pleasure at the cost of disobeying the Lord. And so they chose the things of eternity over the things of this fading life. They chose to obey God over earthly comforts; they chose their heavenly country over an earthly one. They chose these things in faith.

Here is a massive understatement: heaven is much better than Earth. Every problem that we face on this earth is the result of the fall, but in heaven, there will be no curse, no death, no sorrow and no pain. Heaven will be beautiful beyond our imagination, but the best part of heaven is that God Himself will dwell among us. There will be no need of sun or moon because the glory of God will illumine it all the time. The city of God will be perfect because God will be in it. He will walk in it, and manifest himself in every part of it. All that is good, and beautiful, and holy, and peaceful, and true, and happy will be there, because God will be there. And it will never deteriorate. In fact, it will shine brighter and brighter as eternity stretches out into unending ages of increasing joy. We in Christ are going there. The call is to live like you believe it.

This is almost too much to fathom. It's like two toddlers trying to discuss how a computer works. It's impossible for them to grasp. Just like how we can't begin to understand what it will be like in the heavenly country. As Christians, we know it is indescribable and thus we can rejoice, but it will be even greater than our wildest imagination. The patriarchs desired this better heavenly country. *Desire* means to stretch for, to yearn for, to lunge for and to seek after something eagerly and earnestly.[63] The something they sought after was heaven.

Does that describe you today? Do you live like it? Are you heavenly in your affections? If you are, then in faith you despise all things below in comparison with the kingdom of God. As Thomas Watson said:

> We look upon the world but as a prison and we cannot be much in love with our chains. Our hearts are in heaven. And while we are here for a time, our desire is chiefly after the kingdom of heaven, where we shall be forever. So while this world is our temporary home, it's not our delight, how could it be when we have a better, a heavenly country waiting? This is the temper of a

---

[63] Louw, vol. 1, 290.

> true saint; his affections are set on the kingdom of God, his anchor is cast in heaven, and he is carried there with the sails of desire.[64]

Well said. The faithful ones understand this. One newspaper article tells of a young man who once found a five dollar bill on the street, and so from that time on he resolved that he would never lift his eyes while walking. The paper went on to say that over the years he accumulated, among other things, 29,516 buttons, 54,172 pins, 120 pennies, a bent back and a miserly disposition. He also lost the glory of sunlight, the radiance of the stars, the smiles of friends and the freshness of blue skies.[65] Sadly, many Christians are like that man, where they are so engrossed with the things below that they give little attention to the things above. Where we spend all our time seeking after buttons, pins and pennies and we ignore the things that truly matter, the things of God, the things that last, the things of our true homeland. What a waste. Lord help us to look up in faith. Lord help us to be so desirous of what's above, of what lies ahead, that we don't care about all those other fading things that are here below that don't truly matter.

In verse 16 we learn two amazing truths about the Lord. First, that God is not ashamed to be called their God. This is amazing. When God appeared to Moses at the burning bush, He said, "I am the God of your father, the God of Abraham, the God of Isaac, and the God of Jacob." And even though these men were far from perfect, God was pleased to be identified with them. Does that mean that he is proud to be called their God? Yes. Why? Because He has done something for them and for us. He made them a city—the heavenly city, "... whose architect and builder is

---

[64] Thomas Watson, "The Lord's Prayer", Grace Gems, accessed 5/4/2020, https://www.gracegems.org/Watson/lords_prayer4.htm
[65] "Looking Down", Colossians 3:1-2, Bible.org, accessed 5/21/2020, https://bible.org/illustration/colossians-31-2

God." He's not ashamed to be called their God because He has done something for them, not the other way around.⁶⁶ He didn't say, "I am not ashamed to be called their God because they made a city for me." No, but the good pride of God in being our God is rooted first in something he has done for us. And He explained why in the first part of verse 16: "They desire a better country, that is, a heavenly one. Therefore, God is not ashamed to be called their God." The word *therefore* signals the reason for why he is not ashamed, and the reason is their desire. They desire a better country, heaven, the city God has made for them.

That desire calls attention to the superior value of what God offers over what the world offers. In other words, the reason God is proud to be their God—and our God—isn't because we have accomplished something so great. No, it's because He has accomplished something great, and we desire it. It's like getting hungry when you are shown a delicious meal. That is what the city of God is like.⁶⁷ Of course that desire leads us to live out our faith like the patriarchs did, but it all flows out of that desire and love from the heart. Who are we? We are those who are filled with desire, intense desire for home. That desire then compels us to live out that desire, full of faith and Godly action. God is not ashamed to be called the God of those people. As John Piper said, "Open your eyes to the better country and the city of God and let yourself desire it with all your heart. God will not be ashamed to be called your God."⁶⁸ Oh how I want that to be true of me and you.

I want Him to be so proud that He would say, "That's my child. That's my son or that's my daughter. I am the God of Jon Kile."

---

⁶⁶ John Piper, "The Unashamed God," Desiring God, accessed 8/22/2020, https://www.desiringgod.org/articles/the-unashamed-god
⁶⁷ Ibid.
⁶⁸ Ibid.

That would be amazing. Where's your desire? Does your desire show in how you live out your faith today? God is not ashamed to be called their God.

The second truth about God is that He has prepared a city for them. Note that the better country and the prepared city are the same thing. Jesus Himself said in John 14:2, "In my Father's house are many mansions, if it were not so, I would have told you. I go to prepare a place for you." Notice that it is spoken of as prepared because God did it; God appointed it. And He not only prepared this city for us, but He has made all the provisions for us to get there in Christ. Faith allows us to live like we believe all of this in growing measure. Faith allows us to have the passion, the love and the desire of the patriarchs, which compelled them to live for that which is eternal. May our faith grow to be more like that.

CHAPTER 9

Winter 2002:

Have you ever had to go through a serious test? Christians face tests of faith all the time, and our call is to pass those tests. I started preaching when I was 22. It wasn't pretty, but the wonderful people at that little mountain church in east Tennessee were very patient and gracious. As I grew and learned, I knew that the only way I was going to truly please God as a pastor and preacher was to commit myself to expository preaching. Because the Word of God is powerful and effective, the way I was going to become a powerful and effective pastor was to preach the Word with passion, clarity and conviction. Previously I had been using the Word, but now I was committed to actually preaching the Word—what it meant when it was written and then driving home its implications for our lives today—expository preaching.

I made a commitment to expository preaching in the middle of my first full-time ministry. By the time I moved on to my next ministry in California, I was committed to expository preaching regardless of the cost. This was my calling by God, and it was a conviction that I would not and could not compromise.

When I began this ministry, I committed to simply preaching the Word and letting the Word mold the church. It was not long after, that I decided to preach through the book of Romans. The church needed a great theological base, and Romans was the perfect book to give it. Soon the Word began to raise issues that had been previously ignored, such as sin, wrath, original sin, salvation by grace alone, predestination and the sovereignty of God. While many who had previously been in the church struggled with some of these doctrines, others were hungry for the truth of the Word of God.

It wasn't long before the elders received a letter from the previous pastor accusing me of changing the foundation of the church. He began pressuring the elders to fire me. I met with the elders regarding this letter, and there was much discussion. They wanted to end the meeting by telling me, "If a controversial subject comes up again, preach both sides of the issue." I was stunned. For an expository preacher, this was like asking me to compromise my very soul. I told them I couldn't compromise the Word. In my disbelief in what I was being told, I sought to understand, from the elders' perspective, what biblical passage could be called into question, what part might fall under the requirement of preaching both sides? But there was no real answer from any of the elders.

Because they couldn't pinpoint any examples of where they saw this coming up in the future, I stayed and continued to preach. The former pastor's letter had a ripple effect throughout the congregation. The majority of the church had no idea what was going on, but a small group within the church didn't like what I was preaching.

A few months later another issue arose regarding the role of women that had been previously ignored by the former pastor and elders. We examined the Scriptures and faced the problem, and in the midst of that, one of the women on staff quit. At that point the floodgates opened up. The gossip began, the mob formed and soon the elders were being influenced by the group. Lies were told, gossip spread, half-truths abounded, and many people thought things about me that weren't remotely true.

I remember one meeting in particular where a group of men from both in and out of the church met with me and the elders. Once again, the purpose was to convince the elders to fire me. One man called me a liar, another said he would not leave his children with me. There were others who claimed that I had no integrity, and others just made things up out of thin air. Less than a week later, not one of our elders wanted me to stay at the church. It was heartbreaking, it was devastating and I felt completely betrayed. I had considered some of these men close friends of mine.

During that period, there were at least two letters circulated about me that were absolutely untrue. So many things were spread about me during this time, things that the elders knew were lies, but they never bothered to correct. Almost 20 years later, there are still people out there who believe things about me that are false. Was it worth it? Yes, faithfulness to God and His calling is always worth it. Tests of the faith are all around us. Our call is to look to God and to be faithful regardless of the cost. He is always worth it.

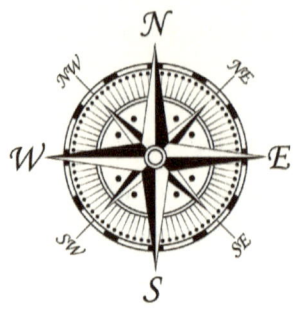

Faith Principle 15
Abraham: The faithful pass the test

A good illustration often brings clarity to the point that is trying to be conveyed. That's what the writer of Hebrews is doing in the next couple of verses in order to encourage us in our faithfulness. Look what he writes in Hebrews 11:17-19:

> By faith Abraham, when he was tested, offered up Isaac, and he who had received the promises offered up his only begotten son, of whom it was said, "In Isaac your seed shall be called," concluding that God was able to raise him up, even from the dead, from which he also received him in a figurative sense.

We have already looked at Abraham, but here, one event stands out that is a shining example of what faith looks like in the lives of God's people. Genesis 22 records this amazing event:

> Now it came to pass after these things that God tested Abraham, and said to him, "Abraham!" And he said, "Here I am." Then He said, "Take now your son, your only son Isaac, whom you love, and go to the land of Moriah, and offer him there as a burnt offering on one of the mountains of which I shall tell you.

The first thing we see is that God tested Abraham. This is made clear in verse 1 of Genesis, and also in verse 17 of Hebrews 11. The Genesis narrative suggests that Isaac was at least 15 to 17 years old, and perhaps as old as 20. In verse 5, Isaac is called a lad, but that term could refer to someone who was up to 20 years old.[69] So Isaac wasn't a young child, but he had the power to resist Abraham if he had so willed to do. My belief is that Isaac was about 15 or 16 years old at this point.

So, what happened? It came to pass, after many years of silence, that God severely tested Abraham. My translation says *test*, other translations say *tempt*, but please understand that God is not tempting Abraham to do evil, for He would never do that. The Hebrew word used here literally means to test, to try or to prove.[70] And so, God isn't tempting Abraham to sin, but rather, God is testing Abraham to prove his character, in order that God may be glorified.

So after as many as ten years or even more of silence, God broke through and simply called him by name. Abraham knew that this was God talking to him. He answered, "Here I am."

What was Abraham thinking at that moment? We can only speculate, but I doubt that he was expecting what God said next.

"Abraham, take your son, your only son Isaac, the son that you love, and offer him up as a burnt offering."

"Say what, Lord?"

What a test! Think about it. How can a God of wisdom, mercy, justice and love ever command Abraham to offer up his only son as a sacrifice? Infant sacrifice was condemned by God in his law that was to come later, and there's no way that God would ever want parents to make it a practice

---

[69] BDB, 654.
[70] Ibid, 650.

of sacrificing their children. And yet, God says, "Abraham, offer up your son."

Note that this was a clear command by God, this was clearly the Word of God, this was something that was undeniably from God and Abraham knew it.

Now of course today if someone came up to me and told me that God had told them to kill their son, I would say confidently that it wasn't God who told them that. But for Abraham in his unique position and in his unique time in human history, it was clear. God Almighty had spoken to him. So how do we deal with this? We take it for what it is. I know that in God commanding Abraham to do this, that it wasn't wrong since God can't do wrong. I also know God did the same thing for us with His own Son that He commanded for Abraham, but God actually followed through with it. The point is that if God tells you to do something and you know for sure that it's from God, then you do it. The clear and undeniable way we hear from God today is in God's book, the Bible. The Bible is God's clear voice for humanity, and our call is to learn it, to love it and to live it out. But for Abraham, while it wasn't a written word, it was indeed a clear word from God. Again, what a test.

God will indeed test His children at times. When God tests us, it's not because He is angry with us. And while God will discipline His erring children, His tests are different. Instead, the tests of God are, as a general rule, God's vote of confidence in us. Tests from God are opportunities to come to understand something of the sustaining power of God in the experiences of life. The tests of His are not designed to cause us to fail, rather, the tests of God are designed to strengthen us and our faith and to give more glory and honor to the Lord. The Christian grows in the difficult times. We are perfected through trials.

Notice that God testing us isn't cruel, but it's an act of a good God towards His people for their benefit, and for His eternal glory. This can get confusing. We often think, is this a test? Is this a trial? Is this truly of God? Is Satan tempting me to sin here? What is this? Well, stop trying to figure it out and focus on being faithful through it. You can't control what comes your way, all you can do is seek God's glory through whatever it is that comes your way and be faithful. As Thomas Brooks said:

> What God, our Father wills, is best. When He wills sickness, sickness is better than health. When He wills weakness, weakness is better than strength. When He wills want, want is better than wealth. When He wills reproach, reproach is better than honor. When He wills death, death is better than life. As God is wisdom itself, and so knows that which is best; so He is goodness itself, and therefore cannot do anything but that which is best—therefore remain silent before the Lord.[71]

So, what do we do? We trust Him, we obey Him, and we remain faithful through it all. God said, "Go and sacrifice your son."

Notice how specific God is here. He said, "Take now your son." Think of that. "Your only son." Or as the text in Hebrews says, your only "begotten son." *Begotten* means unique,[72] and while Isaac wasn't literally the only son of Abraham, Isaac was indeed the unique son that God had promised, and whose birth was a supernatural fulfillment of that promise. So, God is being very clear here to Abraham. On top of that, Ishmael is gone at this point, and so it's clear who God is talking about. It is Isaac. "Your only son, the son whom you love."

---

[71] Thomas Brooks, "Father knows best," Grace Gems, accessed 3/23/2020, https://gracegems.org/Brooks/Mute%20Christian%20QUOTES.html
[72] BDB, 402.

This is the first mention of love in the Bible. Interestingly, it is the love between father and son, and it's clearly connected with the idea of the sacrificial offering of the son. So, what's the point of this? The point is to strip away everything so that God alone is Abraham's focus. God had been building Abraham slowly, bit by bit, year by year, into a man of faith. He had ups and downs and peaks and valleys, but Abraham is growing, learning and moving forward for the glory of God.

In Abraham, we see a picture of what we are called to do as God's faithful children. What comes first, God or your children? God or your job? God or earthly things? God or earthly treasures and riches? God or another person? God must come first, and He certainly deserves it in light of who He is and what He's done for us. Here Abraham is learning the difference between trusting in the promiser rather than the promise. While I am confident that God would never tell any of us today to go and slay one of our children, the Bible is very clear that God must come first in our lives, even above family members, and so it's the same principle. The faithful put God first.

In Luke 9:23, Jesus said, "If anyone desires to come after me, let him deny himself, take up his cross daily, and follow me. For whoever desires to save his life will lose it, but whoever loses his life for my sake will find it." When Jesus said this, it meant that you were willing to pay any price for the sake of Christ, and that you were willing to do that on a daily basis. It meant a daily willingness to endure shame, embarrassment, ridicule, reproach, mockery, rejection, persecution and death for His sake because you love Him so much. It meant that you were willing to start on a death march every day for the cause of Christ if it came down to it. It meant that you would be willing daily to suffer the pains and the reproaches of a condemned criminal for Him if need be. It shows us the absolute priority that Christ must have in our lives over and above anything and everything else. For is anything better or more important than Him? As John

MacArthur noted, "To come to Jesus Christ is to come to the end of self and sin and to become so desirous of Christ and His righteousness that one will make any sacrifice for Him."[73] And this is really what God was asking Abraham to do when He said, "Offer him there as a burnt offering…" In other words, put God first. Don't worship your child, or your spouse, or your money, or your possessions; worship God alone, the only one who is truly worthy of our worship.

I wonder how we would fare if we had a similar test like this. "Kill your son." Or you could say it like this, "Take up your cross daily, and put God first in your life above all else." Same principle. Would you pass or fail? Those who live faithfully pass the test.

In verse 2, God said, "Go to the land of Moriah, and that's where you will offer Isaac as a burnt offering." Note that a burnt offering wasn't an offering that was burned alive, but an offering that was first sacrificed and then completely burned before the Lord. But why did it have to be done in Moriah? Moriah is mentioned in one other place, which is found in 2 Chronicles 3:1, which states, "Solomon began to build the house of the Lord at Jerusalem on Mount Moriah." Isn't that interesting? Mount Moriah, the place where Abraham would offer up Isaac, is also the place where Solomon's Temple would later be built, and consequently, it was the place where thousands of animals would later be sacrificed. It's as if God were saying to Abraham, "Take Isaac, offer him on Mount Moriah, the very place where the animals of the Old Testament will be sacrificed in the temple; those same animals that point forward to the Lamb of God, who will be offered once and for all on that same mountain about 2,000 years later."

---

[73] John MacArthur, *Matthew: The MacArthur Commentary Series*, (Chicago, IL: Moody Press, 1988), 49.

What a picture. In Abraham and Isaac, we see a clear personification of God the Father and God the Son. Abraham represents God the Father, who, out of love for mankind, gave His only Son as a sacrifice for sinners. Isaac then, is a type, a picture of Christ, who submits to the will of His Father. Consider the similarities between Isaac and Christ: Both were loved by their father. Both offered themselves willingly. Both carried wood up the hill of their sacrifice and both were delivered from death on the third day.[74] So this then is a foreshadow of the cross, and it's a beautiful illustration of the infinite wisdom of God and of the inspiration of God's holy Word.

The story continues in verses 3-6:

> So Abraham rose early in the morning and saddled his donkey, and took two of his young men with him, and Isaac his son; and he split the wood for the burnt offering, and arose and went to the place of which God had told him. Then on the third day Abraham lifted his eyes and saw the place afar off. And Abraham said to his young men, "Stay here with the donkey; the lad and I will go yonder and worship, and we will come back to you." So Abraham took the wood of the burnt offering and laid it on Isaac his son; and he took the fire in his hand, and a knife, and the two of them went together.

So Abraham obeyed and went, and in faith he did what God had told him to do. Think about that. Abraham is obedient even though he doesn't fully understand what's really going on. That's real faith. "God says it, I trust Him, I'm going to do it." As we have seen already, real faith is lived

---

[74] David Guzik, 'Genesis 22," Enduring Word, accessed 5/23/2020, https://enduringword.com/bible-commentary/genesis-22.html

out, real faith obeys the Lord even when it's difficult. So Abraham gets up early the next morning. He takes two young men with him along with Isaac. He gets the wood, splits the wood for the burnt offering, takes his son, and he goes. It takes three days to get there, and finally they arrive at the base of the mountain. What was going through Abraham's mind? At this point, Abraham turned to the two young men, and said, "Stay here with the donkey. I and the lad will go yonder, and we will worship."

This is the first use of the word *worship* in reference to God in the Bible. What does the word mean? The Hebrew word here for *worship* simply means, "to bow down."[75] So while Abraham and Isaac weren't going to the mount to have a time of joyful praise, they were indeed going to bow down in reverence and awe to the Lord. *Worship* has been defined as worth-ship, or the recognition of an individual's worth. So, worship of God is expressing back to Him, His worth, which is of infinite value. God alone has infinite worth, and we are at our best when we are expressing our understanding of that infinite worth back to Him in obedience, praise, service and love.

Notice that in verse 5, Abraham says to the two others who were there, "We will come back to you." Why does he say that? Why doesn't he say, "I will come back to you?" Isn't he going there to sacrifice his son in obedience to God? Instead, he clearly says that they will be back. Does this mean Abraham somehow knew this was only a test and that God wouldn't really require this of him?

No. Instead, Abraham's faith is so great that should he follow through with this and kill his son, he believed God would raise him from the dead. He believed this because God had promised that Isaac was the child of promise; that Isaac was the child through whom God would carry on the

---

[75] BDB, 1005.

line of blessing to become a great nation and to bless the world through. That's faith.

So, it is now the third day, and the two of them are going up the mountain. Notice in verse 6 that the wood for the fire is laid upon Isaac, so he is carrying the wood for his own sacrifice. Once again, it's a type, a picture, a living illustration of what Christ would do when He Himself carried the cross that He Himself was going to be sacrificed on.

Abraham took the fire, or the source for the fire, and he took the knife along with him. Note that he didn't forget the knife. I think I would have forgotten the knife. As Spurgeon said, "That knife was cutting into his own heart all the while, yet he took it. Unbelief would have left the knife at home, but genuine faith takes it."[76] And now we are seeing Abraham, the man of great faith. It's all coming to a head and he's still following through. For again, true faith obeys the clear Word of God even when it's hard.

Continuing to verse 7 and 8:

> But Isaac spoke to Abraham his father and said, "My father!" And he said, "Here I am, my son." Then he said, "Look, the fire and the wood, but where is the lamb for a burnt offering?" And Abraham said, "My son, God will provide for Himself the lamb for a burnt offering." So the two of them went together.

Picture them as they head up the mountain, Isaac the teenager and Abraham the old man. They are walking to worship the Lord, to offer

---

[76] Charles Spurgeon, "Spurgeon's verse expositions of the Bible: Genesis: Study Light, accessed 3/25/2020, https://www.studylight.org/commentaries/eng/spe/genesis-22.html

sacrifices to the Lord. Abraham has the knife and the source of the fire; Isaac carries the wood on his back.

And that's when Isaac begins. "My father," the boy starts. After his father's response, Isaac says, "Look, the fire and the wood, but where is the lamb for a burnt offering?"

Now remember what burnt offerings symbolize: total devotion, total dedication to God. The burnt offering was a way of expressing one's heart to God, one's love to God, one's devotion to God and one's commitment to God. Also, it's important to note that sin offerings were pictures of the final sacrifice for sin—Jesus Christ. A burnt offering was totally consumed, which symbolized total dedication. It also symbolized a recognition of repentance and one's sinfulness. Finally, it pictured a sacrifice on behalf of sinners, which pointed perfectly to Christ and His death on the cross in the believer's place. So burnt offerings were important, and it was all a perfect picture of Christ. But here, the offering was to be Abraham's own son.

When Isaac asked his father where the lamb was that they were to sacrifice, Abraham answered the only way he knew. "Son, God will provide for Himself a lamb to offer up." And they continued on. Abraham didn't know how God would provide this, but he knew God would work this out regardless, even if it meant raising Isaac up from the dead. He knew what God had commanded, so he trusted, and he left the rest up to God. Verses 9-10 continue:

> Then they came to the place of which God had told him. And Abraham built an altar there and placed the wood in order; and he bound Isaac his son and laid him on the altar, upon the wood. And Abraham stretched out his hand and took the knife to slay his son.

So in faith, Abraham is about to follow through and offer up his son. They finally arrive and Abraham must now build an altar, using rocks that are scattered all around. Can you imagine? He picks a spot and then starts gathering rocks. Because he's an old man, he has to make several trips, back and forth with his arms full. He arranges the biggest rocks at the base to make it stable. He makes more trips to gather what he needs. Each time he returns, Isaac is waiting for him. Do you think he took his time? When the altar reached the right height, he would level it off to where it was flat, and then spread the wood across the top for the fire. Oh, the agony.

Finally, Abraham has to speak to Isaac. He has to tell his son that he's the sacrifice, that he has to slay him. He has to tell him because he has to bind him up and lay him on that altar. Amazingly, Isaac is a willing victim at this point. Think about it. He's a teenager who easily could have overpowered his old father, but he doesn't. "Not my will but yours be done father." And again, in this we see a living picture of the willingness of Christ to be slain for us.

So picture it, the father's announcement of what he is going to do, the sobs, the kisses, the signs of affection between the father and the son, and then finally the binding of the young man, and placing him upon the altar. Oh, this is heart wrenching. So, Isaac is bound and now he is on that altar. Abraham stretches out his hand, takes hold of the knife and he raises it in faith, ready to follow through with God's command. And just as he is about to plunge the blade into Isaac's heart, look at what happens. Verses 11-14:

> But the Angel of the Lord called to him from heaven and said, "Abraham, Abraham!" So he said, "Here I am." And He said, "Do not lay your hand on the lad, or do anything to him; for now I know that you fear God, since you have not withheld your son,

> your only son, from Me." Then Abraham lifted his eyes and looked, and there behind him was a ram caught in a thicket by its horns. So Abraham went and took the ram, and offered it up for a burnt offering instead of his son. And Abraham called the name of the place, The-Lord-Will-Provide; as it is said to this day, "In the Mount of the Lord it shall be provided.

Isn't this amazing? Just when Abraham is about to kill his son, that's when God intervenes. The angel of the Lord who is Christ, calls out from heaven, "Abraham."

Good timing. "Yes Lord."

"Don't do anything. For now I know you fear God since you have not withheld your son from me."

I think Abraham passed this test. This brings up a question. Didn't God already know the outcome of this? Yes, of course. But it was a good lesson for Abraham, and it's a great picture and lesson for us today of what God did for us, and of what true faith and obedience is to look like. For the best evidence of our faith and love for God is our willingness to serve and honor him with that which is dearest to us, and to be willing to give up all for Him. Real faith and love are seen in sacrifice; not when it's easiest, but when it's the hardest.

I love how God graciously intervened, and then God provided the ram for the sacrifice. The ram was caught in a thicket. Abraham took the ram, killed it and offered it up instead of his son. There are some great Biblical truths in this. For example, as already alluded to, there is the voluntary death of Isaac. We have no evidence that Isaac resisted it at all. And in this, he is the perfect example of the Lord Jesus who willingly offered himself up as a sacrifice for us. Also, in the substitution of the ram for Isaac, the son, we have the doctrine of substitution, where a ram dies in place of the son. For us as believers, Christ died in our place as our substitute for sin.

So yes, Abraham passed the test, God intervened and the sacrifice of the ram was made. Abraham then called the place "The Lord will provide." That is aptly named. For in the fullness of time God would indeed provide the ultimate lamb to die for man's sins, just as He provided a ram to take Isaac's place on the altar. For there on that mountain, and not far away, is where, over 2,000 years later, the ultimate provision was made, when Jesus died as the believer's substitute for sin. The Lord will provide. Yes, He most certainly will. He certainly did.

In our passage in Hebrews, the focus is on Abraham's faith, his obedient faith in the Word of God. How does this apply to us? Here's how. When God's Word commands us to do something difficult, in faith we are called to obey promptly without dispute. That's what real faith does. It may be the command to stay in a difficult marriage, even though you would find great relief in leaving. It may be the command to love a difficult person, or to forgive someone who has greatly wronged you. There are many difficult commands like this in the Bible, and we won't grow in faith if we ignore them. Instead, we must submit to God with prompt obedience if we want to go higher in faith. Also, Abraham surrendered to God the thing that was most precious to him. That's what true faith is willing to do. It would have been much easier for Abraham if God had said, "I'm going to take your life." True faith puts God first above all else.

Our text in Hebrews uses three phrases to hammer home how difficult it was for Abraham to offer up Isaac. First, it refers to Abraham as "he who had received the promises." God had repeatedly promised to make of Abraham a great nation. Abraham and Sarah had waited 25 years, from when he was 75 years old until he reached 100, for God to give them Isaac, the son of the promise. But now, He tells Abraham to kill him. That is not easy in any way.

Second, as we have already seen, the text says Abraham "was offering up his only begotten son." Abraham had fathered Ishmael, and he would have other sons through Keturah, but only Isaac was his unique son, the son of the promise. It's the same term John uses of Jesus, who is God's unique Son (God Himself, the second Person of the Trinity) in a way that no one else is or could be. Offer him up. That is not easy.

To further emphasize the difficulty of this, verse 18 recites the promise, "In Isaac your descendants shall be called." This must have been confusing to Abraham. Before Isaac's birth, Abraham had asked God to let Ishmael be the son of the promise. In Genesis 17:19, God refused, saying, "No, but Sarah your wife will bear you a son, and you shall call his name Isaac; and I will establish My covenant with him for an everlasting covenant for his descendants after him." So now that Abraham has Isaac, God says, "Offer him as a burnt offering." Nothing was more precious to Abraham than Isaac, and now God asks Abraham to kill him.

What's the point? That God should be more valuable to me than even the most precious gifts that He has given to me—even my wife, even my kids, even my things, even my comfort and everything else. This is what real faith looks like, and the call is to be growing in it more and more for the glory of God. Real faith puts God first, for nothing is more important than Him. God wants the absolute first place in our hearts even if it means offering up Isaac. It's a severe test of our faith when He takes something precious from us. Will we, like Abraham, obey with total surrender or will we find fault with God? Real faith persists even when it's hard, rough, painful and bleak. God will provide. God loves me. Heaven lies ahead. God is good no matter what. He saved my soul; He knows what He's doing, and I trust Him no matter what. Faith.

Note how verse 19 in Hebrews 11 says, "Abraham concluded God was able to raise him up, even from the dead." Abraham's faith in God was so great that he thought, "If God wants me to kill Isaac, then to keep

His promise, God will have to raise him from the dead." This is amazing in the fact there had been no resurrections from the dead in world history. The Greek word translated *concluded* means to consider in light of the facts.[77] In other words, Abraham didn't blindly take a leap of faith here. Instead, he considered God's attributes and character. God is loving, just and mighty. He never deceives us. He is faithful to keep His covenant promises. He had promised that in Isaac, Abraham's descendants would be numbered. Isaac didn't have any children at this point, and yet God now had asked Abraham to sacrifice Isaac. Therefore, God must be planning to raise Isaac from the dead. Abraham clearly knows God. Abraham knows the character of God. This shows us how to work through any trial of faith that we encounter. Satan will try to get us to doubt or deny some aspect of God's character or attributes. He got Eve to doubt God's goodness by implying that God was keeping back something good, in forbidding her to eat the fruit. He sometimes tempts us in times of trial to doubt God's love. Don't listen to his lies. That's why Paul affirms that no trial can separate us from God's love in Christ. Sometimes Satan tries to get us to doubt God's sovereignty, suggesting to us that a good and loving God wouldn't permit the kind of trial that you're going through. In faith, we need to refuse to listen to those lies and fall back on what we know about God. Fall back on faith.

With Abraham, faith says, "Even though my current situation seems to go against God's love and goodness, based on His promises to me, I trust He will work it all together for good for me. Even if I die from this, God is still good. I'm going to trust Him to the end for He's never let me down, and my last day here is my best day anyway. I trust Him, and I won't let present hard circumstances steal that trust." Faith.

---

[77] Kittel, 284.

The last phrase, he "received him in a figurative sense" points us to the real reason that God commanded Abraham to kill his own son: that it was a type of what God Himself would do with His Son on the cross. So, we learn from Abraham's amazing faith, and we also learn how amazing our God is, how much He loves us and what He's willing to do to save our undeserving souls. Unlike Abraham, God actually followed through with the killing of His only begotten Son. He followed through out of His great love for us. How could we not love Him back by living faithfully for His glory and pleasure, like Abraham?

CHAPTER 10

John Muir Trail:

Even though the John Muir Trail was incredibly beautiful, it was also, at times, incredibly mundane—like life sometimes. The call? Keep going. After five days on the trail, I grew to hate Clif Bar energy snacks. Blowing up my air mattress every evening and pumping water to drink throughout the day was like torture. My backpack had a squeak in it from the way it rubbed on one of my straps, and that squeak nearly drove me crazy. On top of that, I was so tired most of the time that my brain wasn't always functioning correctly.

One morning, after a tough uphill climb, I stopped for a brief rest when I saw someone walking up the trail. As he came closer, I nodded and offered a tired, "Hey." Instead of walking on, the fellow stopped in front of me and stared. I thought, "This isn't good, there's a crazy guy staring me down." He then said, "Jon, it's me." It was Dave and I didn't even recognize him. Not good. I was really tired. Keep walking.

There was one other time, around day eight, where I had been hiking alone for several hours. As usual, I was exhausted and when I came around a bend, what I saw stopped me like I'd run into an invisible barrier. Just off the trail rose this huge stump of a redwood that must have been struck by lightning because its top half had blown apart and couldn't be seen anywhere. The base rose at least 30 feet high and on top of it sat Dave, looking like a big gargoyle staring down at me. I inadvertently stepped back and did a double take, and when I looked back up Dave was gone. Not good. Now I'm seeing visions of Dave in trees. I was really tired. Keep walking.

It was the 11th day and I had just come off another pass and was heading downhill. I usually like going downhill, but because I was so tired all the time on this hike, the effort going downhill was almost as much as going uphill. The grade started off steep but eventually leveled out a bit as it continued for several miles. I felt my steps grow sluggish as weariness overtook me, forcing me to stop numerous times over the next few miles. Finally, I made it to a creek where a number of people were sprawled out and resting, doing their best to recuperate and refuel with whatever snacks they could find in their backpacks. I remember thinking, "That seems like a marvelous idea." I found a spot to unload my gear next to a group of strangers who were laughing as they traded trail stories. I slipped off my pack and joined the conversation as I fumbled around for my jug to get water. One of the hikers moved closer. "Jon, what are you doing, it's me." I was talking to Dave again and I didn't recognize him. Oh man, I was so tired. I got some water, pulled one of those nasty Clif Bars from my pack and downed it, and then continued on.

The Christian life is like that sometimes. You are weary, you are beaten down and you can barely keep going. The call: keep going in faith and never quit.

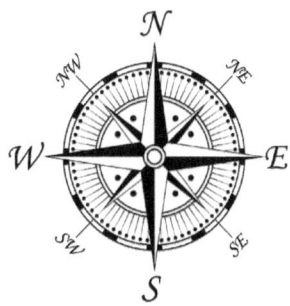

Faith Principle 16
Isaac: The faithful repent and bow to the providence of God

In Hebrews 11:20, Isaac is held up as an example of faith. "By faith Isaac blessed Jacob and Esau concerning things to come." This is interesting because you wouldn't think that a lot could be said about Isaac's faith since so little is written about him. In Genesis chapter 27:1-4, we see more clearly what particular event the writer of Hebrews is alluding to:

> Now it came to pass, when Isaac was old and his eyes were so dim that he could not see, that he called Esau his older son and said to him, "My son." And he answered him, "Here I am." Then he said, "Behold now, I am old. I do not know the day of my death. Now therefore, please take your weapons, your quiver and your bow, and go out to the field and hunt game for me. And make me savory food, such as I love, and bring it to me that I may eat, that my soul may bless you before I die."

Esau then left, and while Esau was out hunting, twin brother Jacob had taken an animal skin, put it over himself so he would feel like his brother. "For Esau was hairy, but Isaac was a smooth man." He then came to Isaac with food that Rebekah had cooked and attempted to deceive blind Isaac. And he did indeed succeed in order that he may receive the blessing instead of his brother.

Verse 26 continues:

> Then his father Isaac said to him, "Come near now and kiss me, my son." And he came near and kissed him; and he smelled the smell of his clothing, and blessed him and said, "Surely, the smell of my son is like the smell of a field which the Lord has blessed. Therefore may God give you of the dew of heaven, of the fatness of the earth, and plenty of grain and wine. Let peoples serve you, and nations bow down to you. Be master over your brethren, and let your mother's sons bow down to you. Cursed be everyone who curses you, and blessed be those who bless you!" So, Jacob got Esau's blessing.
>
> Now it happened, as soon as Isaac had finished blessing Jacob, and Jacob had scarcely gone out from the presence of his father, that Esau his brother came in from his hunting. He also had made savory food, and brought it to his father, and said to his father, "Let my father arise and eat of his son's game, that your soul may bless me." And his father Isaac said to him, "Who are you?" So he said, "I am your son, your firstborn, Esau." Then Isaac trembled exceedingly, and said, "Who? Where is the one who hunted game and brought it to me? I ate all of it before you came, and I have blessed him—and indeed he shall be blessed."

Notice these last words, "... and indeed he shall be blessed." This is an amazing story. Here, Isaac definitely doesn't seem like a great man of faith, but remember, the writer of Hebrews is pointing out to us areas of faithfulness that we are called to emulate, not the areas that we aren't called to emulate. He's trying to give us examples of how we can live out our faith, and there is one such example in Isaac.

That said, it's interesting to me that Isaac is mentioned here in this great chapter of faith. In Genesis 25:28, it says that "Jacob was a mild man, dwelling in tents. And Esau was a hunter, and that Isaac loved Esau because he ate of his game, but Rebekah loved Jacob."

Did you catch that? First of all, this is bad parenting with favoritism and manipulation going on. But then we also see that Isaac loved Esau because he ate of his game. So, he favored one son over the other because his favorite son brought him meat, and he liked meat. You say, "Oh come on, that's a stretch." But even in the verses that we just read from chapter 27, where Isaac is getting ready to bless Esau, he wants the meal first, and then he will give the blessing. He doesn't say, I will bless you and then I will eat your food. Instead, he says, "I will eat your food and then bless you." In verse 4, Isaac says, "Make me savory food, such as I love, and bring it to me that I may eat, that my soul may bless you before I die." Doesn't it seem that Isaac was overly consumed with food, meat in particular? It's an interesting point.

What else can we say about Isaac? He built some wells. S. Lewis Johnson said that "Isaac is noted for the fact that he generally went places and built wells."[78] But is that what you would want to be remembered for?

---

[78] S. Lewis Johnson, "The Faith of the Patriarchs: Hebrews," SLJ Institute, accessed 6/22/2020, https://sljinstitute.net/general-epistles/hebrews/the-faith-of-the-patriarchs-hebrews/html

He's certainly a believer. That is clear, for only a true believer would be included in Hebrews 11. But he's kind of like the person who has been raised in the church and takes it for granted. He doesn't really know how good he has it, where God is good but not great, where grace is pretty cool but not amazing, where you say, "I love my Lord, but I'm not overwhelmed with His love and with loving Him back." And while there is the fruit of true saving faith, it's just a little fruit, not much fruit, not great fruit that abounds. How sad, and what a waste.

And yet so many Christians are like this. We settle for mediocrity. We love our food, and our things. We love the easy way, and we seek the trouble-free life. We go to church, but we don't get too involved, and we don't really share our faith. We take it easy and just coast through life as Christians. We're not really passionately pursuing Him, and we're not really passionate in loving Him and others for His glory, not really. What a waste. This is no way to live out your Christian faith. You could say that Isaac began well and ended well, but in between he wasn't impressive at all. Yet the in between carries great opportunity to honor your God who saved your soul. The wise and the faithful are those who begin well, end well, and do well in between. They know that life is short and what you do for God lasts forever. Redeem the time for the glory of God, every bit of it, as much as you possibly can. This pleases God and reaps eternal reward.

Note this: Isaac knew that the divine activity was going to be carried on through Jacob. We know that because Genesis chapter 25:22 tells us this fact at the birth of these twin brothers.

> But the children struggled together within her; and she said, "If all is well, why am I like this?" So she went to inquire of the Lord. And the Lord said to her, "Two nations are in your womb, two

> peoples shall be separated from your body; one people shall be stronger than the other, and the older shall serve the younger."

So, the Bible speaks very plainly that the promise is given to Abraham, but that it is to continue through Jacob. Isaac knew that. But even while knowing that the promise is destined to come through Jacob, Isaac still seeks to bless Esau. Even so, it was Jacob the deceiver who he was really blessing. Isaac didn't know that because he was blind and was tricked. He thought he was blessing Esau. And so, in that sense, he not only shows that he preferred Esau, but he also was willing to be disobedient to the promises that he, himself, was well acquainted with.

In this entire narrative we see a picture of lies, deceit, favoritism and sin. The story behind Hebrews 11:20 isn't flattering to any of the participants, except for Isaac's faith regarding things to come. Isaac seemed to be more interested in a tasty meal than in God's prophetic word. Esau was a profane man, who had earlier despised his spiritual heritage for a bowl of stew. Rebekah deliberately deceived her husband and encouraged her son to lie. And Jacob agreed to go along with the lies, taking advantage of his blind father. Can God redeem even this? Can God turn this sin-filled story to show forth His glory? Of course He can.

When Isaac found out what had happened, verse 33 says, "Then Isaac trembled exceedingly and said, 'Who? Where is the one who hunted game and brought it to me? I ate all of it before you came, and I have blessed him—and indeed he shall be blessed.'" Notice these words again, "... and indeed he shall be blessed." So here is a man who tried to alter the channel of the blessing of God and have it come through Esau, rather than through Jacob. But he now knows that he's blessed the wrong person. What would you think a person would ordinarily do in that instance?

Note that the father's blessing involved conferring a double portion of the family inheritance onto the firstborn son, coupled with prophetic words about his future. But there's more to it than that with this family. Indeed, the blessing of this family also involves the blessing of land, a great nation to flow through your seed (Israel), and then that all the people of the world will be blessed through him, which is a reference to Christ. And now Jacob has been blessed through trickery, and Isaac responds, "And he shall be blessed." In other words, he recognized in the midst of it all, the providential hand of God. And this is the indication of Isaac's genuine faith. It's as if now he understands. Of course, now we know all the characters in this story are accountable to God and fully responsible for their own sin. But God providentially used all of that to accomplish His purposes. And now Isaac faithfully bows to the providence of God. The call is to have faith like that.

I can hear Isaac, "I was wrong. Jacob shall be blessed, and so will Esau, for he received a blessing as well. But Jacob will be the one through whom the blessings promised to Abraham will flow." I believe that when Isaac says, "And he shall be blessed," he is repenting and truly moving forward into being a man of great faith once again. This is encouraging. Don't be like him in many ways but be like him in this. When you have done something that is clearly wrong, how do you respond? Do you become defensive? Do you deny it, make excuses for it, brush it off or attack the character of the person who pointed it out to you? Many do, but shouldn't we who love the Lord be grateful whenever someone lovingly points out our sin to us, since our goal is to be men and women of God? Isaac's faith is seen in the response to his sin, and in that area the call is to be like Isaac and trust God.

Have you failed? Have you lived a life of mediocrity? Have you sinned greatly? Do you have regrets in your life? Be like Isaac and repent of your sin, go to God with it, lay it at His feet and then move on with your life of faith. The past is gone, but today is a new day and the wise soul is the soul who lives today faithfully for the glory of God. Stop living in the past, honor God today for today is right here in front of you. You can squander it, or you can redeem it and honor God with it. Redeem it.

The great people of God are those who repent of their sin and move on in faith. We all sin, we all have regrets, we all deal with lust and pride, but the faithful don't focus on that and wallow around in it. The faithful focus on giving God their best. They repent quickly and often, they fight sin to the bitter end, they continue on in Christ and move forward—and they put the past behind them and seek God's face. Isaac is an example for us in this. Be like Isaac.

In the end, Isaac repented, and the writer of Hebrews says he demonstrated his faith concerning things to come. In other words, he believed God for what he didn't receive, knowing that he would receive it. When he faced the end of his life and hadn't received the promise, or the land, or the nation, he nonetheless passed it to the next generation knowing that it was still yet to come, but he did it because he believed God. He repented and then he yielded to God in faith. He submitted to the Lord, he didn't reverse the blessing, but he trusted the Lord, and that is an example for all of us.

Like Isaac, do you trust God concerning things to come? Verse 13 says the patriarchs died in faith, so they ended well, "... not having received the promises, but having seen them afar off were assured of them." This is what Isaac was doing. He trusted God concerning things to come. In other words, he knew that God would keep his promises even though it didn't look like it. Real faith lives in light of the things that are yet to come. Home. Heaven. Glory. In this respect, Isaac got it. It was after Isaac had become an old man when he finally seemed to understand. And note that he still had many more years left to honor God with passion at this point in his life. I pray we get it before we are old men and women. Time is fleeting and soon we will be home.

Faith Principle 17
Jacob: The faithful take God at His Word

The writer of Hebrews now turns his attention to Jacob as our example of faith. It says in Hebrews 11:21, "By faith Jacob, when he was dying, blessed each of the sons of Joseph, and worshiped, leaning on the top of his staff." Jacob is an interesting character. What do we know about him? We know that he was sneaky, wily, undependable, a pretty bad brother and a father who had favorites. That's not good. But even though that is true, Jacob was clearly a saved man who put his trust in God to save him. Throughout his life, we see his faith coming forth.

In Genesis, it seems that every time God appeared to Jacob, it was to correct him and to cause some change in his life. Jacob was that kind of person. We all know people like this. They love the Lord, but it's just so very hard for them to overcome their past, their sin and themselves. And it's very frustrating to see. That said, Jacob sought the Lord and was intent on the Lord being his God. He trusted the Lord for life and protection. That is very good. In this we can learn something: persevere, never quit, never give in, never stop pursuing the Lord, and even when you fall, fall forward in faith. There's so much we could say about Jacob, but the writer of Hebrews moves ahead to the end of his life. It's now time for Jacob to pass away and to pass the birthright on to Joseph by blessing the two sons of Joseph, Jacob's grandsons.

This event is recorded in Genesis 48. At this point, Jacob and all of his sons and their families had migrated to Egypt to endure the famine. Joseph then heard that his father Jacob was ill, and so he took his two sons to visit his aged father. Jacob recalled God's appearance to him, and then he claimed Joseph's two sons for himself as heirs. This basically meant designating Joseph as the firstborn, who received a double portion of the inheritance. The natural firstborn son of Jacob was Reuben, but Reuben forfeited his position by having relations with his father's concubine, and so now, Joseph's two sons each get to receive a full portion of the inheritance.

But look what happened. When Jacob went to lay hands on the young men for the blessing, he deliberately crossed his hands, laying his right hand on Ephraim, the younger, and his left hand on Manasseh, the older, which wasn't expected. This obviously troubled Joseph, who tried to correct his father, but Jacob replied that he knew exactly what he was doing. Jacob then predicted that while both sons would be great, the younger son's descendants would be the greater of the two, and so he put Ephraim before Manasseh.

So how is this an act of faith? This is shown to us in Genesis 48:21. "Then Israel, who is Jacob, said to Joseph, 'Behold I am dying, but God will be with you and bring you back to the land of your fathers.'" See, Jacob knows. He blesses these two grandsons because he knows that God will do what God has promised. Jacob had heard from God, and so Joseph couldn't change his mind, and therefore, he couldn't move his hands. Jacob died in faith, never having seen the results, but he trusted God's Word. That's real faith.

Ephraim and Manasseh were the sons of the second most powerful man in Egypt, Joseph. They had been raised in the most luxurious conditions in the world. No doubt they were personal friends with Pharaoh's children. Servants attended to their every need. They had received the best education available at that time. They were heirs to a huge financial estate. They easily could have succeeded in whatever careers they chose in Egypt. In these circumstances, it would have been natural for a grandfather to bless his grandsons by saying, "May you prosper in Egypt even as your father has prospered. May you amass great fortunes and enjoy the best that the world has to offer. Stay in Egypt and flourish."

But Jacob didn't do that. Instead, Jacob, the lowly shepherd who is a pilgrim in Egypt to avoid starvation in the land of Canaan adopts these two princes as his own and confers on them the blessing of Abraham. A worldly-minded parent could have thought, so what? You're giving them a double portion of the famine-stricken land of Canaan, but you don't own a square foot of it, except for your burial cave. Here in Egypt, they've got everything that anyone could dream of having, and you're giving them a piece of dry ground that you don't even own to give away. Thanks, but no thanks.

But what was Jacob really giving to his grandsons? By faith in God's yet unfulfilled promises, he was giving the boys the spiritual blessings of Abraham, which were far better than the worldly blessings of Egypt. Even though there wasn't a shred of tangible evidence that God would give the land to Jacob's descendants, Jacob believed God's promises and handed this off to his grandsons. That's real faith, and Jacob is certainly ending well. Oh, that we would have faith like this.

Sadly, many Christian parents today hope their children and grandchildren find more success on a material level than they do on a spiritual level. They would be thrilled to hear that one of their children was accepted into medical school or landed a big contract with some great company, but they don't seem to care much about the condition of their child's soul. But none of that other stuff matters if the child doesn't know the Lord. So what if they are basking in Egypt if they are outside of the will of God? So what if they are playing with Pharaoh's children if they themselves are going to hell? Jacob trusts God and he's passing on a great example to his son Joseph, as well as to his two grandsons. The call is to trust God like that. No matter the cost.

Faith Principle 18
Jacob: The faithful worship God

What else about Jacob? He worshipped. Note that Jacob's worshipping on the top of his staff happened before he blessed Joseph's sons in Genesis 47. Indeed, Joseph had heard his father was near death, and so he visited him privately. Jacob then asked Joseph to swear he wouldn't bury him in Egypt, but rather in the Cave of Machpelah with his ancestors in the land of Canaan, the Promised Land. When Joseph swore that he would do so, Jacob then bowed in worship.

What's the point in saying this? To show us an old man whose body is weak, but whose faith is strong in God's promises. The picture here is of a man who dies worshipping God, trusting God, faithful to God. It's a great picture, and this is how I want to end my life; faithfully worshipping. The word *worship* literally means to kiss toward.[79] It speaks of being so in awe of God that you bow down before Him and you throw figurative kisses at Him out of love and reverence. This is now how Jacob feels towards God. Here we no longer see Jacob the schemer, but we see Jacob the true worshipper.

What a great way to end. Worshipping God, full of faith. The patriarchs weren't perfect, but they grew in their faith, and they trusted in God's promises. They knew that something much better awaited them, they looked ahead in faith, and they were enabled to face death with a calm serenity and an enduring hope and faith. How else can you describe Jacob's worshipping God while resting on his staff? So even though he was dying as a poor man in a foreign land, he died full of faith in God's promises. And think about this, he's been enjoying those promises for many centuries now. For death to a believer is our best day. For it's at our

---

[79] Louw, 539.

death that we will trade these rags for eternal riches that will never fade away. Jacob knew this to be true, thus he worshipped.

Is God worthy of our worship? The writer of Hebrews is showing us that no one else but God alone is worthy of our affections, our love, our lives, our hearts and our worship. Everything else pales in comparison. Faith worships God even when things aren't perfect. Even when things are rough. Even when we are suffering. Even when we face death. Faith looks beyond that to Christ. It still trusts Him and lifts Him high. Our hope isn't in this life, but in the next. Faithful souls see that fact and they live like they believe it. This life is but a shadow. Biblically, every soul will live on forever, and the key issue is where will you live after you leave planet earth—in heaven or hell? Real life is about your relationship with God, your eternal salvation. It's about whether you will go to heaven or hell. Whether you have Jesus or whether you still belong to the devil. Whether you have an eternal inheritance waiting for you when you die, or whether you will face wrath when you die because you don't have Christ. These spiritual issues are much more important than how wealthy you are, how big a house you have, what kind of car you drive or what name brand you have on your clothes. In fact, all those external things don't matter one bit, for they are temporary; they all fade, they burn and rot. Faith lives for that which is eternal and worships God in all circumstances. Jacob shows this to us at the end of his life, and he's a great example for us. Finish well. Persevere to the end. Trust the Lord and die worshipping.

Faith Principle 19
Joseph: The faithful look ahead

The writer now moves on to teach us something about the faith of Joseph. It's in verse 22, where he writes, "By faith Joseph, when he was dying, made mention of the departure of the children of Israel, and gave instructions concerning his bones." This takes us all the way to the end of

Joseph's life. He had an amazing life. Remember what happened to him? He was the favorite son of his father, Jacob. He received the coat of many colors from his dad, which made all his brothers even more jealous than they already were. He shared a dream he had with his family that portrayed them as bowing down to him, which made them even more jealous; so jealous that they wanted him dead. An opportunity came where, instead of killing him as originally planned, the jealous and angry brothers sold him into slavery. Joseph ended up in Egypt in the house of Potiphar, where he thrived until Potiphar's wife accused him of trying to lie with her, which was untrue. That accusation landed Joseph in prison for three years. Through it all, Joseph was faithful, he wouldn't compromise, and he didn't dishonor his God. It's an amazing story that encompasses twelve chapters of the book of Genesis. In prison, Joseph interpreted Pharaoh's dream, which freed him and took him to the position of ruling Egypt, answering only to Pharaoh himself. Joseph then wisely stockpiled grain in Egypt to avoid a terrible famine. Later, his brothers came to Egypt to buy food, and after many tests, Joseph revealed himself to them. Joseph forgave them, then sent for their father, Jacob, and the rest of his people. They came to Egypt and settled in land that Pharaoh gave them, the land of Goshen. And so out of much adversity, Joseph saved the twelve tribes of Israel. He said to his brothers, "What you meant for evil, God meant for good." In the end, he not only forgave his brothers, but he trusted God through it all. What an example of great faith in the Lord.

Hebrews 11:22 skips all of that and takes us to the end of Joseph's life. Here, Joseph talks about how someday the children of Israel will leave Egypt, and how on that day, he has instructions concerning his bones. Both things refer to the same incident. Why is this event mentioned about Joseph as an example of his faith, when the writer could have mentioned a number of things where Joseph displayed great faith in the Lord throughout his life?

The reason is that it shows us a man facing death at a time when God's promises seemed unlikely to ever be fulfilled. God had given the promises to Abraham more than 200 years before, but here were his descendants living in Egypt, not in Canaan. They were doing quite well in Egypt at this point, thanks to Joseph (and God's sovereignty), but their horrible enslavement in Egypt would follow his death. And then think about this: it would still be more than 400 years before Moses would lead them out of Egypt, and then 40 years after that before they would enter Canaan. Yet Joseph made mention of the exodus out of Egypt, and then ordered that his bones be taken with them when they left. How did he know this would happen? Because God said it, and he believed it even though it seemed unlikely from a human standpoint. He trusted God.

By giving the special instructions about his bones, he was disassociating himself from all of his success in Egypt and associating himself with God's people and promises. It's not about this life, and Joseph knew that in faith. Joseph didn't want a grand tomb in Egypt. He didn't want to be put in a pyramid. He didn't want future generations of Egyptians to come and pay homage at his grave. He wanted his final resting place to be in the land of God's promise. And his burial instructions were a strong exhortation to his people, to not be satisfied with the blessings of Egypt. They should only be satisfied with God's promises for the future.

Sure enough, when Moses finally led the children of Israel out of Egypt, they took all their belongings, knowing they were not returning. With them, they brought unleavened bread, gold and jewelry, furniture and cooking pots, and a box of old bones. Those bones were a testimony to Joseph's faith as he lived in God's assurance for the future. How many years of his life had Joseph dwelt in the land of promise, in Canaan? Six or seven years. That's it. He's now at the end of his life, but those six or seven years in the land had marked him. He was of the children of Israel, and he had faith, strong faith in the One true God. He told his family, "Carry up my bones from here." He's looking ahead, for the patriarch's faith is not directed towards the past, their faith is directed toward the fulfillment of the promises. "Look what God has done and look what lies ahead." The call is to live in light of that. To live well, and to die well, full of faith. You will never regret that, even if it comes with a price in this earthly life.

Today we have the privilege of being able to look back at the Lord's sacrifice on the cross for us. As amazing as that is, let's not forget to look forward. Let's not forget that the Word of God is filled with the promises of the glorious future you and I have in Christ. Cast your anchor of faith in heaven, cast your anchor of faith in the God who saved you and in the God who never deceives. Live for that which lies ahead. These people trusted God and they believed God for what they couldn't see, all the way to death. Yes, they were sinful, and yes, they struggled, but they trusted God and what He had said to them. They died trusting God, even though they never saw the promised blessing themselves. The call is to have faith like them; to live in faith, to die in faith, to die worshipping, and to look ahead through it all.

CHAPTER 11

Chandler Arizona:

My brother goes to a solid, Bible preaching, Christ centered church. When I was at The Master's Seminary, one of my fellow students was pastoring a church in the Phoenix area. A year later my brother got transferred to that area and I told him about my friend. Phoenix is a big area, but the church was in the same area where my brother and his family were moving, and they immediately began attending. They have thrived spiritually in that church for the past number of years.

My brother recently told me about a tragedy that occurred in their church to one of their faithful families. While the family was on vacation, the father, Josh, accidentally ran over his 5-year-old son, Caleb. It seems that Caleb had dropped something in front of the truck and was attempting to retrieve it. That's when Josh pulled forward and his son was killed. After realizing what had happened, Josh and his wife performed CPR until medical professionals arrived. Their son Caleb was taken to glory when he was 5 years,

9 months, and 20 days old. What a heartbreak. Their response to losing their precious son shows us some things about faithfulness as they looked to God for peace and comfort.

In a letter to their church, they wrote these words:

> We dare not question His love. How could we? Rather, we cling to Him. We know God is sovereign, and there is no better place for us than where He has us today. We TRUST! We YIELD! We mourn! We BLESS His name! And though our tears fall almost constantly, we fall on our faces and worship! Blessed is the name of our Lord!

That is what true faith looks like. The faithful trust God even in the face of terrible tragedy. They take God at His Word, and they continue to worship Him, looking ahead to all His amazing promises and remembering that it's not really about this life.

Two months later, Josh wrote a follow up letter to the church. Here is some of what he wrote in that letter:

> The Lord has been exceedingly faithful to us. We have not found it difficult to trust God in this trial. The gospel has been so near to our hearts. And in light of the sacrificial love of God giving His Son as the perfect atoning sacrifice for our sins, we cannot question His goodness, wisdom, and care for us as His children.
>
> The joy of the Lord has been and continues to be our strength. And so, we press on with sorrow in our hearts, tears often in our eyes, and an unwavering joy and hope found in our precious Savior. The sorrow of these temporal days is overshadowed by the hope of eternity with our Lord and the reality of the eternal life we currently possess in Him.

God's Word continues to be more precious to us than all else in this world. It has been a glorious light on this dark path the Lord has set before us. It has revived our souls often in moments of weakness. It has been a shield for us from sinful thinking. When temptations have arisen to want a worldly explanation as to why or how this accident took place, God's Word has abundantly satisfied every curious impulse of our hearts.

God is good. That doesn't change because of our circumstances. We are sad a lot but not discontent. We are committed to worshipping God amid our sadness. We have resolved to let each moment of sadness be a catapult of worship for the gift Caleb was. We are worshipfully and dependently embracing with thankfulness God's good plan for our family. In our sadness, sorrow, and frequent tears, there is also joy and hope. God is faithful! We are vessels created for God's good pleasure to bring Him glory. We will not stipulate what that must look like. Rather we will embrace His perfect plan, entrusting ourselves to Him and seeking to live out His purpose for our lives to glorify Him.

Once again, this is a living example of what faithful living looks like in the lives of God's children. The faithful continue to worship God, even in the face of tragedy. They trust Him and His good providence even when bad things happen, and they continue to look ahead. The next few verses in Hebrews show us these truths.

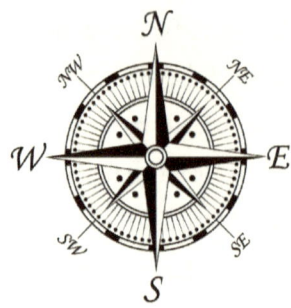

Faith Principle 20
Moses' parents: The faithful don't fear

The writer continues to teach us about faith by looking at the parents of Moses in Hebrews 11:23:

> By faith Moses, when he was born, was hidden three months by his parents, because they saw he was a beautiful child; and they were not afraid of the king's command.

Here we continue to learn about true Biblical faith. Up to this point, the writer has done a great job at not only defining and explaining true faith, but also at showing us what it looks like. He has shown this to us through the lives of some of the faithful in the Old Testament: Abel, Enoch, Noah, Abraham, Isaac, Jacob and Joseph. The writer now turns to the faith of Moses, specifically, the parents of Moses. As we look at them, we find that true faith isn't afraid. True faith casts aside fear and continues to do what's honoring to the Lord. In other words, fear doesn't stop you from living out your faith.

Remember the story? The Israelites were slaves in Egypt, and pretty soon, the slaves were getting so numerous that the population explosion was becoming a threat to the Egyptians. So Pharaoh gave the decree that all male babies were to be drowned in the Nile River. And so, in order to protect their newborn son, Moses' parents, Amram and Yohebed, hid their infant son for three months. Can you imagine trying to hide a newborn baby for three months? Especially knowing that if you get caught, not only is your baby going to die, but you also will most likely die a terrible death. But even so, despite the consequences, the passage tells us Moses' parents hid him because "they saw that Moses was a beautiful child." Some people have differing opinions about what this means, but I think their motivation was more than just the fact that their newborn baby looked good! Every parent thinks their child is beautiful, but clearly there is more going on here.

In Acts 7:20, Stephen, just before he is martyred for his faith, talks about Moses, and he says that when Moses was born he was well pleasing to God. I believe that Moses' parents somehow knew that God had a special plan for this particular child and thus they acted. Philip Hughes believed that the parents saw Moses' beauty as a promise of future blessing and believed that God had chosen him for some great purpose, and would therefore preserve his life.[80] Peter Lombard believed that Moses' parents must have seen something in this baby boy to make them hope that he would be the promised deliverer of his people, and so, because they thought that God had destined him for such a great role, they defied the king's edict and hid him for three months.[81] Whatever the case, it seems clear that the parents knew that God wanted them to hide their child. So they did, risking their own lives to save their baby and to do the will of God. We look at this and say, "Who wouldn't do that?" Well, evidently many didn't at that time, but Moses' parents did as an act of faith in God.

Exodus chapter 2 tells what happened. Verse 1:

---

[80] Philip Hughes, *The Epistle to the Hebrews: New International Commentary of the New Testament*, (Grand rapids: MI: Eerdman's Publishing Co, 1977), 492.
[81] Ibid.

> And a man of the house of Levi went and took as wife a daughter of Levi. So the woman conceived and bore a son. And when she saw that he was a beautiful child, she hid him three months. But when she could no longer hide him, she took an ark of bulrushes for him, daubed it with asphalt and pitch, put the child in it, and laid it in the reeds by the river's bank. And his sister stood afar off, to know what would be done to him. Then the daughter of Pharaoh came down to bathe at the river. And her maidens walked along the riverside; and when she saw the ark among the reeds, she sent her maid to get it. And when she opened it, she saw the child, and behold, the baby wept. So she had compassion on him, and said, "This is one of the Hebrews' children." Then his sister said to Pharaoh's daughter, "Shall I go and call a nurse for you from the Hebrew women, that she may nurse the child for you?" And Pharaoh's daughter said to her, "Go." So the maiden went and called the child's mother. Then Pharaoh's daughter said to her, "Take this child away and nurse him for me, and I will give you your wages." So the woman took the child and nursed him. And the child grew, and she brought him to Pharaoh's daughter, and he became her son. So she called his name Moses, saying, "Because I drew him out of the water.

This is truly a story filled with drama that clearly shows us the providence of God. Note how God orchestrated everything. Moses' real mother gets to nurse him, she will get paid to do it and she doesn't have to hide it. But the key here is that because of their faith, Moses' parents were not afraid of the king's command, and so they acted in faith and did something that could cost them their lives. But even so they did it, and they entrusted their situation to the Lord. In other words, they looked at the fear of death and probably torture and said, "We will not give in to you. We will not kill our son out of fear for our own lives. The fear of death will not control us. We trust the Lord, and we're going to do what God wants us to do even in the face of death." The call is to have faith like that.

Imagine how carefully they had to live. If the baby cried at any time of the day or night, they had to muffle him while they tried to calm him down. I'm sure they couldn't risk having their children play with other children in the neighborhood for fear that they would let something slip about their baby brother. And then think about this: if Pharaoh's men roamed the neighborhood looking for newborn baby boys, the family would have sat in silent terror. They all could have been slaughtered because of what they did. Pharaoh had ordered all Hebrew parents of baby boys to take their infants and throw them into the river.

Although it would have been agonizing, they could have rationalized it by saying, "What else could we have done? We probably would have been caught and our whole family would have died. On top of that, he would have lived a miserable life as a slave like the rest of us. We were doing him a favor by throwing him into the river." Sounds good, but what about what God thinks?

In faith, Moses' parents chose to obey God and risk the consequences. They feared the unseen God who is the author of life more than they feared the king's edict of death. And there we see more of what true faith is all about—that even when there is reason to fear, that fear will be controlled through faith in God. Faith demonstrates trust in Him, and it emboldens the Christian to do what's right no matter what.

So here's the question: are you going to live in fear or are you going to trust the Lord and do His will despite that fear? Sadly, too many Christians live in spiritual fear instead of faith. They are afraid to stand up, so they bow down. They are afraid to speak up, so they remain silent. They are afraid to do what's right because it's not always easy, so they do nothing. They fear their situation more than they fear God. Instead of doing what's right and trusting the Lord with the consequences, they become Christian cowards who live in mediocrity and compromise. Where's the faith?

You say, "But Jon, if I stand up against the sin at work and if I tell them I can't continue to lie and cheat for them, I might get fired." Then get fired. "But Jon, if I don't give in to the crowd at school, I'll be made fun of and laughed at. It's easier to just give in." Life is filled with choices. Do you want the approval of people or of God? It's better to be made fun of and please God, than be popular and displease Him. Faith pleases God.

Real faith says, "I'm going to do what's right no matter what because I trust the Lord." The call here is faithful obedience that walks where Christ would have us walk. Not selective obedience that comes only when it's easy, but obedience to His will at all times and in every circumstance. Obedience, even when your life is on the line. Obedience, even when it may hurt, even when it may cost something. Obedience, when you may lose some friends, when you may lose your job, even when you're mocked. Obedience even when your family turns against you. True faith trusts God and obeys Him despite the consequences.

In a previous ministry, I was talking to a couple who were interested in becoming Christians. They had heard the good news and they were excited about becoming Christians. But they told me they had a problem. If they became Christians, they would disappoint their family and their family might disown them. Sadly, they ended up rejecting Christ for their family. They gave in to fear to their own eternal detriment. I remember when I was in Seminary, I was in a class where we started talking about the persecution of Christians throughout the ages. One guy, a preacher, said that if he was a Christian during a time of persecution and they came for him, that he would have no problem denying Christ because that way he could live longer in service to the Lord. But where's the faith in that? And what about all the lovers of God throughout the ages who refused to deny Christ because they loved Him so much, and who died because of it? This man was rationalizing sin and cowardice, and he definitely wasn't displaying the faith described here in Hebrews 11. Fear says compromise; faith says obey God. Fear says give in; faith says live it out no matter what. Fear says take the easy way; faith says take God's way even when it's harder.

Here, the writer is telling us, "Don't be afraid. Don't tremble with alarm as a Christian. Don't be intimidated. Don't be scared. Don't shrink away as a coward, but stand strong, be bold and courageous for Christ."

As a Christian, what really is there for us to fear in this fading life? We know what is ahead. We know that to die is gain and that we ultimately win. We know that heaven is our real home. And we know that we have an eternal inheritance that is waiting for us. So again, what's there to fear?

The writer of Hebrews points to something special in 13:6, "The Lord is my helper I will not fear, what can man do to me?" Long before that, Isaiah 50:7 says, "For the Lord God will help me; therefore I will not be disgraced, therefore I have set my face like a flint, and I know that I will not be ashamed." And then, Psalm 27 starts off, "The Lord is my light and my salvation, whom shall I fear? The Lord is the strength of my life, of whom shall I be afraid?" In Acts 5:29, when accused by the high priest, the chief priests and the captain of the temple, Peter and the other Apostles respond, "We ought to obey God rather than men." They didn't allow the threats of man to terrify them. They knew in faith, that pleasing God was more important than fearing men. True faith does what's right even in the face of fear. God is certainly worth it. Be like Moses' parents.

CHAPTER 12

2015:

True faith is seen when things get hard. Will you stay faithful when your faith really costs you something? Back in 2015, I witnessed something on television that was both horrific and shocking: the day on a beach in Libya when a group of 21 orange-clad men were beheaded for their faith.[82] Twenty of the men were Coptic Christians from Egypt, while the 21st named Matthew was from West Africa. He too was a Christian. His captors actually told him that he could go free. However, he said, "I am a Christian." He chose to share in the fate of the others. The demeanor of all 21 men was amazing. They looked peaceful as they made their way to their deaths, clearly eager to see their Lord. Their last whisper in death was, "Oh my Lord Jesus."[83]

---

[82] Stoyan Zaimov, "21 Coptic Christians Beheaded by ISIS Honored for Refusing to Deny Christ," Christian Post, accessed 1/12/2022, https://www.christianpost.com/news/21-coptic-christians-beheaded-by-isis-honored-refusing-deny-christ.html

[83] ibid

Apart from Matthew, the other twenty men were Coptic migrant workers from Egypt who came from poor farming families and had travelled to Libya to find better paid work. In Libya, they had been sleeping side by side on the floor in a large room so they could save more money to send home to their families.[84] They were ordinary men, but they had great faith. They knew that God was worth glorifying to their dying breath.

For the last 1,400 years, their people had been a minority, often oppressed and downtrodden. Their outsider status had helped preserve their greatest treasure: their Christian faith. These men had been refined by their trials, and they had been well-prepared to stand strong in the face of death. As one young woman who knew them said, "They were ready to die, and even longed to. We all do. We're all ready and yearning because we all want to vouch for Christ."[85] This is the way of faith.

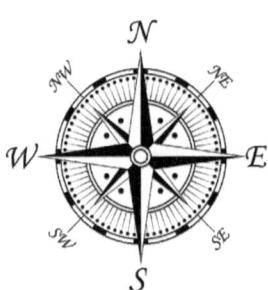

Faith Principle 21
Moses: The faithful choose suffering over sin
In verses 24-26, we see more great principles of Biblical faith:

---

[84] ibid

[85] ibid

> By faith Moses, when he became of age, refused to be called the son of Pharaoh's daughter, choosing rather to suffer affliction with the people of God than to enjoy the passing pleasures of sin, esteeming the reproach of Christ greater riches than the treasures in Egypt; for he looked to the reward.

Here we find when Moses was 40 years old, he faced a decision; he could either become a full-fledged Egyptian, or he could join his own people, the people of Israel. Remember, for 40 years Moses had been a prince of Egypt. During that time, Egypt was the greatest, wealthiest, most cultured society around, and Moses could have had it all. In fact, he did have it all, and he could have kept it all. How many people today would love to have been Moses? How many today would have sold their soul to be in Moses' position? Power, prestige, riches, being called the son of Pharaoh's daughter and all the privileges that go along with that? Jewish tradition tells us that Moses had great prospects of actually gaining the throne of Egypt. We're not sure if that's accurate, but it could have been his reality. Indeed, Moses faced a huge decision. He could accept everything that the physical world could offer, but to do so would require he turn his back on God and God's people. Or he could throw in his lot with the despised Israelites, give away wealth beyond imagination, and become a member of that insignificant band of slaves who lived in misery, but knowing that this was where God wanted him. From Stephen's speech in Acts 7, we learn that at this time, Moses knew in his heart that he had a mission to perform for God. He knew what God wanted him to do. Even so, he struggled with what to choose and the ramifications of that choice: the world and all its delights, or God and slavery?

Take a moment to consider such a decision if the choice was yours. A life of fame is desired by many. So many people are enchanted by those with a claim to fame. For some reason, the world accepts that famous people belong atop a pedestal, whether an entertainer, an athlete or simply someone born into the lap of luxury and wealth. This world envies the famous, idolizes them for what they have, and would trade most anything to experience their own fifteen minutes of it. This world stumbles all over itself to be a part of the world of the famous. Then there is the lure of money, which can bring power and prestige, big houses and a cache of toys at every age. It sometimes buys love because to the wealthy, love often turns into a commodity. Wealth announces your name in lights. Nearly everyone hungers for the fame of the wealthy; they'd do anything to experience it.

And yet Moses renounced it all. He turned his back on all these trappings and willingly chose suffering over sin. Moses knew what God wanted him to do so he did it. He deliberately chose a life of suffering and hardship over a life that embraced ease, sin, indulgence and every earthly pleasure. That's true faith. The faithful are like that. It's a faith, a trust in God that declares, "I love the Lord, and I'll seek to do His will whatever the cost, even if it means I have to suffer."

While many Christians do anything and everything to avoid suffering, Moses chose it. He walked into it, in faith and for God's glory. He said, "I'm going to leave the palace and live among the slaves because that's what God wants me to do. I'm going to leave my riches and suffer because that's what God wants me to do. I'm going to leave the pleasures of the world and choose pain because that's what God wants me to do." What a great man of faith.

Notice that the writer of Hebrews mentions "...the passing pleasures of sin." This shows us that Moses knew sin brought pleasure for a moment, but pleasing God lasts forever. He knew sin starts with a lie and brings misery, and that suffering for God is better than any fading pleasure that sin can offer. Satan lies behind sin, and sin will always leave you miserable in the end. And Moses knew this. He knew the truth, and so Moses decided by faith for the things that are imperishable, the things that last forever, the things that truly have eternal value. He chose to obey God; He chose to please God and to suffer. True faith always chooses to be faithful to God even when it means suffering. How's your faith today? Do you love God enough to suffer for Him? Do you love Him enough to leave your sin and all its fading pleasures behind you? We often don't really know the answer to this question until faced with the test. We must, however, prepare to make the right choice by making God our center.

Look at John the Baptist. John had a calling from God, and so he renounced himself and he lived for God. He lived in the desert, he ate locusts and wild honey, he was clothed with camel's hair and a leather belt, and he was basically a wild man for God. John preached the truth, and the truth he preached offended many people. He called the hypocrites a brood of vipers, he lived to please God at all costs, and when it got him thrown into prison, he didn't compromise. When Herod was living in sin; Herod the one person who could free John, John spoke out against this man's sin, and when John lost his head for doing God's will, that's the moment that John knew it was all worth it as he passed from this life into the next life in glory. That's what true faith is: it doesn't back down, it doesn't grow slack, it can't be bought off, it can't be wooed by sin, and it trusts even in the face of suffering. It runs away from sin and into the lion's den—if that lion's den pleases God. Why? Because we love and cherish God more than anything else in this fading life. "I love Him more than my sin, I love Him more than worldly pleasure. I love Him more than I love you and your approval. I love Him above all else, and so I'll live faithfully for Him, and I'll die faithfully for Him." Faith keeps this love at the forefront of our minds and lives.

Faith Principle 22
Moses: The faithful esteem reproaches over riches

In verse 26, it says, "Moses esteemed the reproach of Christ greater riches than the treasures in Egypt." Here we find that Moses believed the worst he could endure for Christ would be more valuable than the best of the world. That word *esteemed* involves careful thought,[86] and so we see that Moses carefully thought through the decision he had to make, and when he weighed everything out, he knew that reproach for Christ was much better than worldly riches.

It's interesting that the writer uses the word Christ here, since Moses lived nearly 1,500 years before Christ. What does the writer mean by this? He means that Moses knew God had promised to raise up a prophet like him who would speak His Word (Deuteronomy 18:15). He knew of God's promise to Eve, that One from her seed would bruise the serpent's head (Genesis 3:15). He also knew that the sacrificial system pointed ahead to a redeemer. And so, it seems clear that Moses considered any reproach that he endured for identifying himself with God's Messiah, was far more valuable than the worldly treasures he could amass in Egypt. In faith, Moses looked forward to the Messiah. He identified with the people of God, with the Messiah's people, and what he did in faith definitely pleased Christ the Messiah, his coming deliverer. For the glory of Christ, the Messiah, God the Son, Moses esteemed reproaches over riches.

That word *reproach* means to revile, to blaspheme and to slander.[87] So, Moses said, "I'd rather face that for Christ's cause, for the coming Messiah's cause, than face a world of riches and go against Him. I'd rather be hated and reviled by people and give up wealth and possessions and everything else in order that I may please my God." And he did. True faith

---

[86] Bauer, 343.
[87] Kittel, vol. 5, 238.

sees beyond the things of this world and looks to the heart of God. It asks, "What do you want me to do Lord? You're the one I long for. You're the one I love. You're the one I want to please. These things don't mean a thing, so what do you want from me Lord?" And then faith lives it out. For true Biblical faith is focused on God and doesn't get sidetracked by temporary things.

This is really a heart issue, for true faith longs and hungers for God. True faith looks into the face of God and everything else just fades away. True faith thinks about what God Almighty has done for you; how Jesus died for you when you were His enemy. True faith is captivated by Him out of your love for Him. As in Psalm 42:1, true faith says, "As the deer pants for the water brooks, so pants my soul for you, O God." This is the way of true faith. The person with true faith is motivated and captivated by his intense love for God and doesn't get sidetracked by the trivialities of this fading life.

Faith Principle 23
Moses: The faithful look to the reward

The writer of Hebrews continues to extol Moses' faith by telling us at the end of verse 26, that Moses looked to the reward. The reward here isn't any earthly reward, for Moses walked away from all of that. Instead, the reward here is the heavenly reward. So the object of Moses' quest wasn't something physical, but it was something eternal. His heart wasn't set on the things of this earth, it was set on heaven and on the God of heaven. Heaven was his real home because heaven was the home of his God, and that's what Moses longed for, that was his true motivation. That's what our motivation should be as well. In faith, Moses looked for the reward, and the reward was being with his God forever in heaven. That's what Moses wanted most; to be in the presence of the God he loved and longed for. Faith looks ahead and lives in light of that.

Think about it, Moses chose a course that he knew would bring him the world's reproach. Why would a man knowingly choose such suffering? Because he was wise. Like the man who sold everything he had to buy the pearl of great price, Moses gained something much better, the reward.

True faith counts on eternity. In the short-term, Moses had to endure ill-treatment with a bunch of refugee slaves in the wilderness. But in light of eternity, as Paul put it in Romans 8:18, "...the sufferings of this present time are not worthy to be compared with the glory that is to be revealed to us." He also wrote in 2 Corinthians 4:17, "For momentary, light affliction is producing for us an eternal weight of glory far beyond all comparison." True faith looks to the reward and lives in light of what's coming. That's what Moses did. Be like Moses.

CHAPTER 13

John Muir Trail:

One of the essential concerns for any long-distance hike is water. Are there regular water sources along the trail, and how many miles are there between those water sources? This is important because running out of water on a hike is both miserable and dangerous. The good news is that the John Muir Trail has tons of water sources since much of the trail follows alongside rivers and passes by lakes. There are only a couple of places along the trail where water is a problem.

Not only do you need good water sources, but you also need a way to purify your water. For our John Muir Trail hike, Dave and I had two ways to purify our water: a SteriPen and a pump. A SteriPen is a small device that uses a short wave germicidal ultraviolet light to purify water. To use it, we would simply fill our water bottles in a stream, slip the SteriPen into the water bottle and press a button to turn the light on. We'd stir the pen around in the bottle for 90 seconds, and after that the water would be good to drink. The only problem with the gadget was the batteries which drained quickly, and even though I'd brought extra, they ran out halfway through the hike.

The water purification pump was our other resource for safe water. Even though the water pump was bigger than the SteriPen, it worked quickly and easily. You'd simply pump the water out of the lake or stream into your water bottle, and you'd be good to go.

While there were many times on the trail when I came close to running out of water, there were only two times when it actually happened. For the hike, I carried two water bottles with me. When one of the water bottles was empty, that's when I would start looking for a water source to fill up. Most of the time there was water nearby, but sometimes I would get about halfway through the second bottle before I would come across water.

The first time I ran out of water was going up one of the many mountain passes on the trail. There were usually a number of lakes or streams along the trail, but not this time. Halfway up the pass is when I emptied my first water bottle and began looking for a water source. By the time I got to the top of the pass I was completely out of water and very thirsty. As I began walking down the pass, I could see a couple of lakes in the distance, but they were miles away. Not good. About a mile down the trail, I came up to a small lake. The lake was off the trail a couple hundred yards, but it was down a pretty steep ravine with a bunch of boulders between me and the lake. I had no choice. I took off my pack, grabbed my SteriPen and water bottles, and crawled over a bunch of large sharp boulders to the lake. Ahhh, the water tasted amazing. Getting back to my pack wasn't fun, but what choice did I have? Water is necessary.

The second time I ran out was much the same as the first. This time, I had come down a pass and had miles of relatively flat, mundane hiking. I was very tired, and I think that's why I didn't pay attention to the fact that I only had half a water bottle left. No big deal, right? There's plenty of water. Nope. I soon ran out of water and was getting desperate. I finally came across a small, smelly, ugly lake that was off the trail. I normally would have passed on getting water here, but I was truly desperate. I could tell my body was shutting down. My head throbbed, I hadn't gone to the bathroom for hours and I was getting severely dehydrated. I knew the SteriPen would kill anything that would make me sick, but the water still looked and smelled horrible. I filled my water bottles, used my gadget, held my nose and drank the water. Better than nothing right? I was very happy to have it.

Water is essential. About every other day after we'd set up camp, I would go down to whatever steam we were next to and dip my towel into its icy water and cleanup from all the caked-on dirt and grime I'd picked up on the dusty trail. It felt so refreshing. I made it a habit of dipping my hat into every creek or stream that we crossed, and it always revived me. There's something comforting about the sound of water going over rocks that is soothing, and as I said before, it sounded like actual singing more times than I could count. The light of the moon reflecting off the still surface of a lake late at night was absolutely breathtaking. You not only need regular water sources to survive on a long hike, but the water of rivers, lakes and streams makes a long hike much more enjoyable.

This fact made me think often of Jesus. Jesus said to the woman at the well that He is the living water. Just as water is essential for physical survival, so is Jesus essential for eternal life. What are we left with without Him? He alone gives hope, peace, forgiveness, joy and life. The faithful understand this. "Jesus is my living water. He is my all in all." Their lives reflect that understanding.

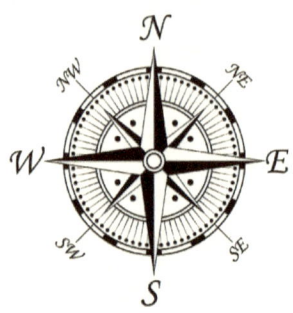

Faith Principle 24
Moses: The faithful forsake the world for God's pleasure

Hebrews 11:27, referring to Moses, says, "By faith he forsook Egypt, not fearing the wrath of the king; for he endured as seeing Him who is invisible." This is an interesting verse because it's hard to tell exactly when in the life of Moses this is referring. Remember, Moses had it all for 40 years, but even with all the luxuries and worldly things, something wasn't right. Moses knew that he was really a Hebrew. He knew who his true people were, and he also understood he would have some kind of role in bringing about his people's deliverance. So, at this stage in his life, things are coming to a head for Moses. Stephen's speech in Acts 7:23 says this:

> Now when Moses was 40 years old, it came to his heart to visit his brethren, the children of Israel. And seeing one of them suffering wrong, he defended and avenged him who was oppressed, and struck down this Egyptian. For he supposed that his brethren

> would have understood that God would deliver them by his hand, but they did not understand.

I think this is the event where it all was laid out for Moses; either side with the Egyptians or side with God and the Israelites. Choose God and the suffering that will be a part of that life or choose sin and Satan. Be rich on earth or be rich in heaven. When Moses stepped in and defended his fellow Hebrew and killed the Egyptian, the choice was made. The next day, Moses went out and he saw two Hebrew men fighting and Moses said to one of them, "Why are you striking your companion?" The man replied, "Who made you a prince and judge over us? Do you intend to kill me as you killed the Egyptian?"

Exodus 2:14 says, "Moses feared and said, 'Surely this thing is known!'" Pharaoh then sought to kill Moses, and Moses fled into Midian, where he lived for the next 40 years of his life.

The issue is this: our verse in Hebrews says that it was "by faith that Moses forsook Egypt and that he didn't fear the wrath of the king." But there in Exodus, it tells us that after the killing of the Egyptian became known, Moses feared and then fled for Midian because Pharaoh sought to kill him. If that's the case, then it doesn't seem like Moses was acting out of faith. It seems like Moses was acting out of fear. This could pose a problem. There are some commentaries that state verse 27 of Hebrews isn't talking about when Moses was 40 and he left Egypt, but about when he was 80 and led the people out of slavery into the wilderness. They say that when Moses left Egypt and went to Midian, he went out of fear. They say that when he was 80 years old, he went back and led the Israelites out of slavery, and it was at that time he left Egypt in faith.

I disagree. I believe it's clear that verse 27 is talking about when Moses was 40 because it fits with everything that we've already learned about Moses and his great faith up to this point, and chronologically it fits with the passage. Ultimately it doesn't really matter when this happened, but even so, I believe this happened when he was 40 years old. Specifically, I believe it was when he chose to defend his fellow Hebrew and kill that Egyptian.

John Piper puts it like this:

> Yes, he had experienced fear when the word spread that he had killed the Egyptian while saving a Jew, just as his parents had experienced fear when they saved their baby boy and risked their own lives. But hiding their baby was not an act of fearful, self-serving unbelief, and Moses' leaving Egypt was not an act of fearful, self-serving unbelief either. It was a preserving, an enduring in spite of fear in the obedience of faith. He wasn't driven merely or mainly by fear, but he looked to the unseen God to work out some purpose for his people, and 40 years later he would discover what that purpose was, and he would be back.[88]

I agree, and I think Moses forsook Egypt before he was threatened by Pharaoh. From what we've already learned about the faith of Moses, he certainly wasn't one to flee unless he believed that fleeing was the thing that God wanted him to do. And while I think Moses was afraid when the killing of the Egyptian became known, I don't think he was driven by that fear. It's clear that if Moses believed it was what God wanted him to do, he would have stood up and died at the hands of Pharaoh. But I also believe Moses knew it wasn't his time. He knew God had a plan, and he knew the thing to do at that moment was to go to Midian. And so he went

---

[88] John Piper, "Faith Makes the Difference When we Walk Through Crisis," Desiring God, accessed 4/14/2020, https://www.desiringgod.org/messages/liberated-for-love-by-looking-to-the-reward

in faith, believing that this was God's will. This certainly fits with what we know about Moses.

Faith Principle 25
Moses: The faithful see Him who is invisible (Part II)

Regardless of the exact timing, the clear point is that Moses was a man who saw Him who is invisible, and he lived in the light of that reality. In other words, Moses lived as if God was right there visibly in front of him. Because of his faith, he looked into the face of the God who he couldn't see, and he saw Him. He fixed his eyes on the invisible God, and even though Moses couldn't see God, his faith allowed him to see. Out of faith, Moses lived as if God were right there with Him at all times in every place, and his life reflected that reality. "Even though I can't see Him, I know He's there. Even though I can't reach out and touch Him, I know He's watching. I know that God is alive and real. I believe what I do matters to Him, that I will give an account of my life to Him, that He's here and I will live faithfully with that reality in mind." This is what faith means.

Because of that fact, Moses was able to forsake Egypt. He was not overrun by fear, and he was able to endure. He saw Him who is invisible through his eyes of faith. Think how much better off we would be if we could live like God was visibly with us in the circumstances of our lives. He definitely is with us, but not many Christians live like they believe that. Again, just think about if we really saw Him who is invisible, and if we really believed that God was with us in every circumstance of our lives. Would we live differently? Would we be so quick to compromise out of fear of people's approval? Would we hold so tightly to the fading things of this world? Would we care so much what other people think? Would we be so quick to give in to the lust, the anger and the temptation? Wouldn't we stand up for truth more? Wouldn't we hold our tongue more? Wouldn't we share our faith more?

We could use a good dose of faithfully seeing Him who is invisible, because too many Christians live like He's not really there. But He is. God is watching, God is with you, God sees all and God knows all. It's wise to live in the light of that truth.

An illustration in 2 Kings 6:16 fits here. It's there that the prophet Elisha is in a certain city, and the city is surrounded by enemies. Elisha's servant is struck with distress, and Elisha says, "Do not fear, for those who are with us are more than those who are with them." Elisha then prays to God, "Lord, open his eyes so he can see." The Lord then opens the eyes of Elisha's servant, and that's when he sees all around them the mountain is full of horses and chariots, God's heavenly armies.

We need to remember that while we may not see God and His heavenly hosts, they are alive and real, and God really is right here. In faith, Moses lived like he really believed it. That truth ought to give us strength, encouragement and confidence. It also ought to make us think twice about giving in to that sin, that temptation, that thing that dishonors the one we love. True faith realizes this truth and lives accordingly.

Faith Principle 26
Moses: The faithful obey (Part III)

Moses has just endured the wrath of the king, but now he has to be saved from the wrath of God. Verse 28 says, "By faith he kept the Passover and the sprinkling of the blood, lest he who destroyed the firstborn should touch them." Remember what happened? In Exodus, chapter 12, at the culmination of the plagues, God instructed Moses on how Israel was to observe the Passover. The other nine plagues had come and gone, and still Pharaoh wouldn't allow the Israelite slaves to go and worship God in the wilderness. So, by the mighty hand of God, the blood came, along with the frogs, the lice, the flies, the livestock disease, the boils, the hail, the locusts and then the three days of darkness—a darkness so dark that it could be felt. Pharaoh still said, "No, I won't let you go." Then the tenth plague came. In it, came the death of the firstborn of all the people and animals. Note that this was a plague on both the Israelites and the Egyptians. The plague involved the firstborn being killed on a certain night. To avoid the punishment, the people were to kill a lamb and then paint the lintels and door posts of their houses with the blood of that lamb. God warned the people that He would go through the land on that night and kill every firstborn male in the homes that didn't have the blood of the lamb on the doorposts. And that's what happened. For Moses and the people to be spared, they needed the blood of that Passover lamb applied to their doors. What an incredible foreshadowing of Christ.

The New Testament is very clear that Christ is our Passover Lamb who was slain for us who believe (1 Corinthians 5:7). The whole Passover event was a picture of Jesus who was to come and die on a cross so all who believe could be saved from the wrath of God against our sin. Jesus died so we who believe can live; Jesus shed His blood and died as our substitute so we can be forgiven and be forever with God. Jesus our Passover.

It's now the night of the first Passover; the night of the tenth plague. In a very real sense, the blood of the lamb saved the Israelites' first born from death, as it kept the destroyer from entering their homes. Note that while the children of Israel in Egypt followed God's command and kept the first Passover, none of the Egyptians did. And so, all through Egypt, behind the unmarked, bloodless doorways of the Egyptians, the firstborn children died at midnight. "There was loud wailing in Egypt, for there was not a house without someone dead" (Exodus 12:30). This dire judgment finally changed the Egyptian king's heart, and he released the Israelite slaves. The writer of Hebrews tells us that it was by faith that Moses and the children of Egypt kept the Passover. As we have seen numerous times already, true faith obeys the Word of God.

Notice a few things about this event. Note first, that it wasn't only the Egyptians, but also the Jews who faced God's impending judgment of the death of their firstborn if they didn't apply the blood of the lamb to their doorposts. Being a Jew by birth wouldn't have spared anyone. Being a decent, hardworking person who had never committed a crime didn't matter one bit. While Moses' faith is mentioned in 11:28, his faith didn't cover all of the Jewish homes. Each home had to apply the blood as God had commanded or the family would suffer the dire consequences. This shows us that everyone will answer to God, and your family heritage won't save you. Only Jesus saves through faith in Him alone.

Note also that there were elaborate instructions for how to carry out the Passover. For one thing, it wasn't cheap. Every family had to sacrifice a lamb, or if the family was too small, they could join another family. Along with the instruction to apply the Passover lamb's blood to their doorposts and lintels, God instituted a commemorative meal: fire-roasted lamb, bitter herbs and unleavened bread. It must be done according to the way God told them to do it. Don't miss a step, and don't take it lightly. Carefully obey. For that lamb is going to be your substitute. That lamb is going to die so you can live, but in faith, you have to obey what God says.

Finally, to be delivered, Moses and the Israelites had to trust God's Word and do what He told them to do. If anyone disputed it by saying, "It's not logical that sprinkling blood on our doorposts will protect our oldest child from death," then that person's child would have died. It also wouldn't have been enough to just say, "I believe" mentally, but to not apply the blood. No, to be saved from the destroyer, the person had to believe God's warning and then respond by applying the blood.

The same is true with the blood of Christ. You can argue that God is a God of love, not judgment, and that you don't need the blood of Christ—the death of Christ—to be saved. But you will someday learn too late that He is also a God who judges sinners. Perhaps you grew up in a

Christian home and you believe in a general sense, but you haven't personally fled to Christ in repentant faith. James 2:19 warns us that the demons also believe in that manner, but they will not be saved. Unlike the Passover, it is not enough for your father to believe on your behalf. You must personally believe in Christ as Lord and Savior, for everyone is accountable to God. Therefore, you must personally trust in Christ's blood (His death) as God's payment for your sin, and you must apply the blood of Christ to your heart by faith to be saved from God's judgment. And for Moses and the children of Israel, this was done in faith. The call is to be like them.

Do you trust God? Do you trust the Word of God? Will you obey God even when it doesn't make perfect sense to you? Would you apply blood to your door? In other words, will you trust in Christ alone as Lord and savior? That's what faith does. It believes and it obeys. How deep is your faith? Your obedience will show you that reality.

CHAPTER 14

2010:

My wife Tiffany and I were both shocked and devastated. We knew our beautiful thirteen-year-old middle daughter Emily was struggling, but we had no idea that it was something like this. When she finally told us, it felt like all the air went out of the room. I found it hard to breathe, even harder to think of what to do. I looked around and nothing seemed real, like I was lost in my own house, someone had changed everything, all the furniture was rearranged, the lamps and photographs were in different places. Nothing was as it had been just a short time before. I looked to my wife and found her staring at me, her eyes reflecting my own disbelief. In her expression I saw disbelief and then grief that reflected a hurt to the core, the kind only a parent can feel for their child.

I won't go into the horrible details, but what I will say is that a wicked person had done something terrible to Emily. Our world was consumed in finding a way to deal with this. Our first priority was finding a way to minister to our daughter who didn't want to talk about it. The next couple of years were pretty tough. We took matters to the police, but that eventually came to nothing. We arranged for our daughter to see a Christian counselor, but Emily continued to struggle. We did our best to love Emily, disciple her and train her in the way of the Lord. Tiff excelled at this. Through it all we kept loving Emily, praying for her, sharing the truth of Christ with her and pointing her to the Lord.

I found something that surprised me about myself. I've always known I am a weak man like all other men are, and I am prone to sin as any other man is because of our sinful nature. And as a pastor, I have trained myself to take control of these failures in my life and move forward. But from the first I realized I had to deal with a level of anger that had never been so intense. I found I wanted revenge on the person who hurt my daughter. It has been more than a decade now and yet there is a part of me that still wants retribution against that individual. And the only way I am able to deal with this is in faith. I choose to leave that in the hands of the Lord, for vengeance belongs to him, not me.

How much do we really trust the Lord when things get hard? Will we remain faithful when tragedy strikes? God doesn't promise that nothing bad will ever happen to us as His children because we live in a wicked world—and trust me when I say that this world outside of knowing Christ is truly a wicked world. Will we continue to trust Him through the hardship? Through this ordeal there were a few people who we'd confided in, but not a one was able to really help us during this time. While they loved us and loved Emily, they had no idea what to do or say. But God is faithful, and God comforted us as we drew near to Him.

And Emily? For a long time, the joy that once was evident in our free-spirited daughter seemed to have faded. That distance was understandable as she struggled with everything that had happened. But she always knew that we loved her, and more importantly she always knew that God loved her. And ultimately, that was enough. Today, Emily serves faithfully in her church in Southern California. She leads Bible studies for her friends, she loves her Lord and seeks to glorify Him. And she has climbed over the hurdle that blocked her from being who she was, and through her success she gives hope to all people who have been hurt in their past. It would be naïve to say Emily doesn't still deal with what happened to her, she does—but she doesn't allow it to define her, for God is a refuge and strength in times of trouble. And life is full of troubles. Our hope lies in the Lord and in our faithfully pursuing and honoring Him whatever life throws at us. God is good even when life is painful and hard, and good news, the best is yet to come.

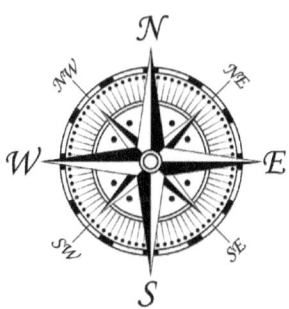

Faith Principle 27
The children of Israel: The faithful step out

We continue to learn about true faith in verse 29. "By faith they passed through the Red Sea as by dry land, whereas the Egyptians, attempting to do so, were drowned." In this verse we have fully moved to the faith of the people of Israel, which is interesting because the author of Hebrews has previously told us, in chapter 3:8-12, the generation that came out of Egypt was evil and unbelieving. The apostle Paul explained that although all Israel passed through the sea, "with most of them God was not well-pleased; for they were laid low in the wilderness" (1 Corinthians 10:5). But here the author indicates they had passed through the Red Sea by faith. How might this be resolved? It seems the best solution is that the faith of the believing remnant, true believers, is generalized to cover the entire nation. Another example is in the New Testament when everyone on the ship with Paul was saved because of Paul's faith, even though they didn't believe in God. Whatever the case, they crossed the Red Sea in faith.

Remember what happened? After the Passover event, Pharaoh said something like, "Go, get out of here, we will all be dead if you guys stay." And so, the Hebrew slaves set off on a journey across an unknown desert, to an unknown Promised Land. It wouldn't be long before the whole power of Egypt would be hot on their heels. Exodus 13:17-18 tells us this:

> Then it came to pass, when Pharaoh had let the people go, that God did not lead them by way of the land of the Philistines, although that was near; for God said, "Lest perhaps the people change their minds when they see war, and return to Egypt." So God led the people around by way of the wilderness of the Red Sea. And the children of Israel went up in orderly ranks out of the land of Egypt.

Verse 21 continues:

> And the Lord went before them by day in a pillar of cloud to lead the way, and by night in a pillar of fire to give them light, so as to

> go by day and night. He did not take away the pillar of cloud by day or the pillar of fire by night from before the people.

Isn't that amazing? All is good for them now, right? No. Chapter 14, beginning with verse 5:

> Now it was told the king of Egypt that the people had fled, and the heart of Pharaoh and his servants was turned against the people; and they said, "Why have we done this, that we have let Israel go from serving us?" So he made ready his chariot and took his people with him. Also, he took six hundred choice chariots, and all the chariots of Egypt with captains over every one of them. And the Lord hardened the heart of Pharaoh king of Egypt, and he pursued the children of Israel; and the children of Israel went out with boldness. So the Egyptians pursued them, all the horses and chariots of Pharaoh, his horsemen and his army, and overtook them camping by the sea beside Pi Hahiroth, before Baal Zephon.

What now? If Israel had stayed in Egypt, they wouldn't be in as much danger as they were at the Red Sea. Some of the unbelievers actually said to Moses in Exodus 14:11, "Is it because there were no graves in Egypt that you have taken us away to die in the wilderness?" That wasn't true. Moses didn't lead them to the dire situation that they were in, God did. And it was by God's direct action that this defenseless bunch of slaves had the Red Sea in front of them and Pharaoh's army charging at them from behind. They were doomed unless God intervened, which He planned to do. They had to learn that salvation is completely from God. For there was no place for human ingenuity or some scheme to escape. No, God led them into this desperate situation to teach them to trust Him as their only option.

Look what Exodus 14:13 says:

> And Moses said to the people, "Do not be afraid. Stand still, and see the salvation of the Lord, which He will accomplish for you today. For the Egyptians whom you see today, you shall see again no more forever. The Lord will fight for you, and you shall hold your peace.

Moses knew. In faith, Moses knew and trusted God. And it was in faith that the people also stepped up to the Sea. Note that throughout Exodus, the people of Israel give us many bad examples but not here, and the writer of Hebrews wants us to be like them in this aspect: step out. Step forward, trust the Lord and obey Him no matter what.

Verse 15 says, "And the Lord said to Moses, 'Why do you cry to Me? Tell the children of Israel to go forward.'" Four verses later in verse 19, it adds:

> And the Angel of God, who went before the camp of Israel, moved and went behind them; and the pillar of cloud went from before them and stood behind them. So it came between the camp of the Egyptians and the camp of Israel. Thus it was a cloud and darkness to the one, and it gave light by night to the other, so that the one did not come near the other all that night. Then Moses stretched out his hand over the sea; and the Lord caused the sea to go back by a strong east wind all that night, and made the sea into dry land, and the waters were divided. So the children of Israel went into the midst of the sea on the dry ground, and the waters were a wall to them on their right hand and on their left.

Can you imagine? Think of taking that first step. Think of walking through the Sea on dry ground with a wall of water to your right and left. What happened to Pharaoh's army? They all drowned. They pursued the children of Israel, but God fought for them. Verse 26 tells us what happened:

> Then the Lord said to Moses, "Stretch out your hand over the sea, that the waters may come back upon the Egyptians, on their chariots, and on their horsemen." And Moses stretched out his hand over the sea; and when the morning appeared, the sea returned to its full depth, while the Egyptians were fleeing into it. So the Lord overthrew the Egyptians in the midst of the sea."

Skipping to verse 30, it says:

> So the Lord saved Israel that day out of the hand of the Egyptians, and Israel saw the Egyptians dead on the seashore. Thus Israel saw the great work which the Lord had done in Egypt; so the people feared the Lord, and believed the Lord and His servant Moses.

This is incredible. Here we have the faith of a leader and of a people who were prepared to attempt the impossible at the command of God. They believed that the greatest barrier in the world is no barrier if God is there to help us over it. This is nothing for God, and neither is anything else. When trials come, when tragedy comes, when hardship comes, when enemies pursue you, you can trust your God with it. That is a certainty. He will see you through, whether by life or by death. "What if I step out into the sea and I drown?" Then you drown in faith. Living faithfully for the glory of God isn't for the faint of heart. We are called to trust Him even when we face great pain, hardship and loss because of our faith in

Christ. We still trust Him. He's the God of all creation, He's sovereign. He loves us more than we could ever imagine, and no matter what happens, God is still good. God is always working for my eternal good as His child, and the question is, will I trust Him with this? Step out, obey, go forward, trust and obey Him no matter what. Many times, He figuratively parts that sea for us and destroys our enemies. And if he doesn't, we trust Him still, and we know that in the end it's all good for us His children. True faith steps forward; true faith obeys no matter what.

John G. Paton left Scotland to take the gospel to the cannibals, and as he was getting ready to leave, an elderly friend of his repeatedly sought to deter him. His crowning argument was always this: "The cannibals! You will be eaten by cannibals!"

Paton finally replied, "Mr. Dickson, you are advanced in years now, and your own prospect is to be soon laid in the grave, there to be eaten by worms. I confess to you, that if I can but live and die serving and honoring the Lord Jesus, it will make no difference to me whether I am eaten by cannibals or by worms. And in the Great Day, my resurrection body will arise as fair as yours in the likeness of our risen Redeemer."[89]

Let's have faith like Paton, and Moses, and the children of Israel, and let's step forward and trust the Lord with our souls and our daily lives. For He is trustworthy.

Faith Principle 28
The children of Israel: The faithful obey (Part IV)

What other examples happened by faith? The walls of Jericho fell down. Verse 30 shows us, "By faith the walls of Jericho fell down after they were

---

[89] John Piper, "Immortal till His Work Was Done: John Paton (1824–1907)," Desiring God, accessed 4/22/2020, https://www.desiringgod.org/articles/immortal-till-his-work-was-done

encircled for seven days." Remember what happened? Just as the people were entering into the Promised Land after wandering in the wilderness for 40 years and just after Moses died, Jericho was the first obstacle of many that Joshua and the army of Israel faced in conquering Canaan, the land that God had promised to Abraham. So how are they going to conquer the first city in the Promised Land? Easy. Overpower the people of Jericho with military might of course. Or this: surround them, wait until they all starve, and then go in. Or how about coming up with some other brilliant military strategy; one that people in generations to come will want to follow because it's so magnificent. Or this: walk around the city once a day for six days blowing rams horns, and then on the seventh day, circle the city seven times blowing trumpets, and then shout. Really? Anything but the last one, because the last one makes no sense. Unless of course this is the way the Lord told you to do it. Well, that's exactly the way the Lord told them to do it, and so in faith, they did it.

For six days the army of Israel marched around the city, one time each day, blowing those rams horns. What did the people feel like when they were marching? What did the people in Jericho think? Joshua 6:15 picks things up for us on the seventh day:

> But it came to pass on the seventh day that they rose early, about the dawning of the day, and marched around the city seven times in the same manner. On that day only they marched around the city seven times. And the seventh time it happened, when the priests blew the trumpets, that Joshua said to the people: "Shout, for the Lord has given you the city!" And then down to verse 20, "So the people shouted when the priests blew the trumpets. And it happened when the people heard the sound of the trumpet, and the people shouted with a great shout, that the wall fell down flat.

> Then the people went up into the city, every man straight before him, and they took the city.

That was an act of great faith. Who does that except those who believe what God tells them? Sometimes faith looks pretty foolish to the outsider, but who cares what the outsider thinks when we know what God says. True faith lives this out regardless of what others might think. Marching your army around a walled city for seven days while blowing trumpets is not a sensible plan for victory. If Joshua had held meetings with his top commanders, none of them would have suggested this plan. So why then did God choose this approach? I think He wanted to teach Israel that true victory comes when we don't trust in ourselves, but when we trust in the Lord. The repeated trips around Jericho served to drive home the lesson, "You can't conquer this city in your strength. You must trust in God's power." It's a great lesson in faith. Often our problem isn't that we are too weak, but our problem is that we think we are strong. God wanted the people to know that it was all Him, and that's good for us to know as well. Trust Him.

Recall the story of Gideon going against the Midianites in Judges 6? He rallied an army of 32,000 men against 135,000 enemy troops, but God told Gideon that he had too many soldiers, not too few. If they won, they would boast in their victory, and so Gideon sent home 22,000 warriors who were afraid. But then God told him he still had too many. Gideon weeded them out until he was left with 300 soldiers. Finally, being weak enough, God could grant them victory and they would give the glory to Him alone.

Do you trust Him? He can give you victory if it's His will. And if it's not His will, then you don't want the victory anyway. Your call is to trust Him through it all.

Clearly faith and obedience are inseparable. The people of Israel could have said, "That's an interesting plan, Joshua, and we believe that God could do it that way. But we're going to try a more sensible approach." That would have been faithless and disobedient. Instead, they had to march silently around the city once a day for six days, blowing rams horns. The seventh day, when Joshua told them to march around it seven times there may have been some groans. Each time around the city took between 30 minutes to an hour for it wasn't a big city, but the seven times took at least three and a half hours. By the seventh day, some could have been grumbling under their breath, "This is dumb. Nothing has happened yet." If that was the case, it's not recorded. The Bible tells us they obeyed what God had commanded and when they shouted, the walls miraculously came crashing down. True faith obeys even when it doesn't make sense. It says, "We trust God more than you, or ourselves, or anything else. We trust God and we will obey Him based on that trust." And that's when walls crumble.

Think about this: Moses, leading two million refugee slaves down to the Red Sea with no way of escape from Pharaoh's army wasn't in line with conventional wisdom. But he did it in direct obedience to God. Taking the same people out into the wilderness seemed like a sure formula for disaster, but God had commanded him, and Moses obeyed.

Worldly wisdom might say, "You can't get ahead in your business by being honest with your customers." Faith obeys God, even if it should lead to financial loss. Worldly wisdom says, "Everyone sleeps together before marriage. How else will you know if you're compatible? Besides, God will forgive." Faith says, "I'm going to obey God. I won't compromise even if other Christians are doing it, because God's word is clear, and I trust Him."

Worldly wisdom says, "Don't forgive that person who wronged you. Hit them back." Faith says, "Forgive and please God because God sees." Worldly wisdom says, "If someone is mean to you then you be mean to them." Faith says, "No, I'm going to love you. I'm going to be gentle, kind, Godly and peaceable to you no matter what." True faith obeys God.

Also consider why God didn't say, "March around Jericho once, blow the trumpet and shout and the walls will fall down." Why drag this on? It's a good question and a good lesson. True faith is patient. True faith waits on God. True faith trusts Him even though the wall is still up. So never give up, never give in, never quit, never stop trusting God to your dying breath; that's the motto of true faith.

True faith doesn't have a limit. "I'll trust God for this long, but then if He doesn't answer my prayers, I'll quit. Or, I'll trust God, but..." No, real faith trusts God through the fire, and it trusts God even when the walls remain after six days, or years, or decades. True faith looks ahead in confidence that God will act in His perfect timing, and I trust and obey Him until that time comes, or until I die and my faith becomes reality.

Note also that there is no record that Joshua told the people in advance what was going to happen. They just knew that he knew what God had commanded, and they obeyed. When he told them to shout, they shouted expectantly, and God caused the walls to crumble. So, faith waits expectantly, knowing that God will act in His power and in His time. Until then, keep marching.

Faith Principle 29
Rahab: The faithful stand alone

Also note this: while Israel was marching around Jericho that week, another drama was taking place inside one house in the city. A prostitute named Rahab was crowded in her house with her extended family, waiting anxiously to see what would happen. Her story is in this chapter on faith, and it is condensed into one verse. Verse 31 says, "By faith the harlot Rahab did not perish with those who did not believe, when she had received the spies with peace."

Can you relate to Rahab? It's easy to miss the point and fail to relate to Rahab. The truth is, we are all spiritual prostitutes who have cheated on God, and we are no better than Rahab, perhaps we are much worse. This reality exalts the amazing grace of God even more on wretched sinners like us. Can God save prostitutes? Can God save adulterers? Can God save liars? Can God save you? Yes.

The story of Rahab is found in Joshua, chapter 2. We are now looking back before Jericho was conquered. In its day, Jericho was the most important Canaanite fortress city in the Jordan Valley. It was a stronghold directly in the path of the advancing Israelites, who had just crossed the Jordan River. Before entering the land west of the Jordan, Joshua sent two spies to look over the land. The king of Jericho heard that two Israelite spies were within his city, and he ordered them to be brought out to him. Rahab, the woman with whom the spies were staying, protected them by hiding them on her roof. She told them how the citizens of Jericho had been fearful of the Israelites ever since they defeated the Egyptians and the Red Sea miracle 40 years earlier. She agreed to help them escape, provided that she and her family were spared in the upcoming battle. The spies agreed to her request, giving her three conditions to be met: 1) she must distinguish her house from the others by hanging a scarlet rope out of the window so the Israelites would know which home to spare, 2) her family must be inside the house during the battle, and 3) she must not turn against the spies later on. The spies then escaped the city safely.

In the end, the city was completely destroyed and only Rahab and her family were spared. Eventually, Rahab married an Israelite man from the tribe of Judah. Her son was Boaz, who was the husband of Ruth. Joseph, the legal father of Jesus, is her direct descendant. Rahab's faith is lifted up to us as an example in verse 31. The call: have faith like Rahab.

From a Jewish perspective, Rahab had three strikes against her: she was a woman, she was a Canaanite and she was a prostitute. Even so, except for Abraham's wife, Sarah, Rahab is the only woman mentioned by name in Hebrews 11. A woman and a prostitute—yet she is held up as an example of true faith. From early times, many commentators have tried to dodge this by saying that Rahab was only an innkeeper. But the Hebrew and Greek words are clear: she was a prostitute. So why did the spies go to a prostitute's house? To hide. There's no sin going on here, for they are simply hiding from the king who wanted to kill them. Such houses were open at night, no questions would have been asked, and the spies went where they could hide the easiest. That said, God's providence was behind all of the spies' reasons for going to Rahab's house. Even though Rahab was an unlikely candidate for salvation, God's grace had reached down to her, and she became a true believer.

Notice that Rahab was perceptive, intelligent and well-informed. Rahab identified the spies for what they were, hid them and had a plausible story. Rahab also gave the two Israelites excellent advice. She told them to hide in the hills for three days before attempting to cross the Jordan.

Spiritually speaking, Rahab wasn't in an ideal circumstance to come to faith in the one true God, the God of Israel. But neither are any of us. Rahab was a citizen of a wicked city that was under God's condemnation. Rahab was part of a corrupt, depraved, pagan culture. Rahab hadn't benefited from the godly leadership of Moses or Joshua. However, Rahab had heard from the many men she came into contact with that the Israelites were to be feared. She heard the stories of their escape from Egypt, the crossing of the Red Sea, the wanderings in the wilderness and their recent victory over the Amorites. She learned enough to reach the correct, saving conclusion: "For the Lord your God is God in heaven above and on the earth below" (Joshua 2:11). It is that change of heart; her faith that was coupled with action that saved her and her family. I believe it was that moment Rahab was saved—not just from the army of Israel but from the judgment of God. Note the fact that she is called "Rahab, the harlot," even after her conversion underscores God's amazing grace toward sinners. God can save anyone, even a terrible sinner like me and you. Rahab is proof of that.

So, God commanded Israel to kill everyone in Jericho. Modern critics, who sinfully think they are wiser than God, believe that God was cruel to order the extermination of everyone in Canaan. But God had given the Canaanites forty years to fill up the measure of their sin. For forty years, they had heard how God delivered Israel from Egypt through the Red Sea. For several years, they had heard how God had defeated the Amorite kings, Sihon and Og, on the other side of the Jordan. For seven days, they had watched Israel march around their city. But they did not repent of their sins. Only Rahab did. Rahab could have complained that God was unfair to judge her city. She no doubt lost many friends in the conquest. But instead, she knew she deserved death for her lifestyle. She knew the Lord God of Israel is "God in heaven above and on earth beneath." Although the entire city trembled with fear of the impending attack, their fear didn't lead to repentance and faith. But Rahab's did and she was saved. That's how it works. Sin must be judged, and God is the judge. And the wise soul is the one who doesn't put God off for another day. Rahab's fear led her to turn from her sin and to believe in God. And by faith, she "did not perish along with those who were disobedient."

Some scholars actually think Rahab had come to faith in God before the spies arrived at her house. And when God providentially brought the spies to her house, she saw it as the means of deliverance for herself and for her family. And although she probably didn't understand much theology, she had enough faith in the one true God to save her. Note that her past life of sin didn't disqualify her from salvation. This is good news for us all. God is very good at saving horrible sinners for His glory.

Those who perished are called those who did not believe, or the disobedient. They were the ones who had heard of God's power, but they refused to submit to Him. They thought that their walled city would protect them from God. To be saved, Rahab had to break away from her people, her culture and her source of income. Although that is never easy and she must have wrestled with her decision, by faith she made the break. True faith makes the break and honors God. True faith means making a distinct break from this evil world so that we often stand out. But so be it, for God is worth it.

Rahab believed and acted. Her faith led her to hide the spies and send them away secretly, even though it put her life at great risk. In faith she also had to obey the instructions the spies gave her to put the scarlet rope in her window and to have all of her family inside the house with her in order for them to be saved, which she did. It may have seemed crazy to them to watch Israel marching around the city thirteen times. But she obeyed and she was saved.

God saved her from physical destruction, and in faith He saved her from eternal destruction. God is very good at reclaiming the lives of the worst of sinners who turn to Him in repentance and faith.

Rahab is used as an example of what true faith should look like in the life of the believer. True faith obeys, true faith steps forward and trusts God in trial and hardship. True faith is willing to look drastically different to the watching unbelieving world as we march around Jericho looking like fools to them. Faith does what God says, and true faith makes a distinct break from the evil world and obeys.

We obey because we love Him, because He is worthy, because we know what lies ahead and because He is our all in all. We obey because now that we have Him, having Him is all that matters. Like Rahab, in confident faith we see the unseen God and that changes everything. May God increase our faith today.

CHAPTER 15

John Huss was born around 1370.[90] His last name literally means goose, and it is from his terrible fate that the phrase "Your goose is cooked" was derived.[91] He became a preacher when he was twenty-two, and because of his relationship to a man of God named John Wycliffe—as well as with his convictions to preach the Word—Huss was excommunicated for faithfully preaching the truth as opposed to the lies that were so prevalent in his day.[92] Huss said that the Bible was the final authority for the church, and soon he was to be tried for his beliefs. Instead of receiving a fair trial, Huss was imprisoned for months, and was eventually brought before authorities in chains and asked to recant his views. If he recanted, he could go free. Instead, he said, "I appeal to Jesus

---

[90] G.V. Lechler, "Hus, John," ed. Philip Schaff, *A Religious Encyclopedia or Dictionary of Biblical, Historical, Doctrinal, and Practical Theology*, (Toronto, New York & London: Funk & Wagnalls, 1894), 1043-45.
[91] Matthew McMahon, "The Reformation," A Puritan's Mind, accessed 8/14/08), http://www.apuritansmind.com /Reformation/Reformation.htm
[92] James Wylie," John Huss and the Hussite Wars," Doctrine, accessed 8/17/09, http://www.doctrine.org/ history /HPv1b3 .htm#CHAPTER%207

Christ, the only judge who is almighty and completely just. In His hands, I plead my cause."[93]

While Huss was speaking and pronouncing these words, he was derided and mocked by the whole council. Afterward, they stripped him of his priestly garments, degraded him and put a paper hat on his head with devils painted on them with the inscription, "A ringleader of heretics."[94] He still refused to recant his biblical beliefs and convictions, and as a result, he was to be burned at the stake. When the time came, the executioners undressed Huss and tied his hands behind his back with ropes. They then tied his neck with a chain to a stake around which wood and straw had been piled up so that it covered him to the neck.[95] The fire was kindled, and as the flames burned, Huss sang, "Christ, thou Son of the living God, have mercy upon me."[96] Huss died because he was faithful to God with his life and calling. Faithfulness is worth it, and the faithful ones understand this.

---

[93] Ibid.
[94] Ibid.
[95] Ibid.
[96] Ibid.

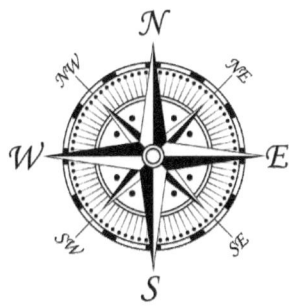

Faith Principle 30
Judges, prophets and others:
The faithful overcome and push ahead

Verse 32 continues to talk about the faith of the faithful. "And what more shall I say? For the time would fail me to tell of Gideon and Barak and Samson and Jephthah, also of David and Samuel and the prophets."

Here, the writer of Hebrews lists seven more men to emulate, and then he also lists the prophets. These people aren't in chronological order, and it's as if he is now just rattling off names that can inspire the original readers and us in our own faith. All these named are people who were saved, but also note there is much in the lives of most of these people that are poor examples for us. As we have already said, we take it the way the writer of Hebrews intended us to take it. We cast aside the times when these people were bad examples, and we use the times when they were good examples of faithful living, and we emulate those.

Several judges serve as examples. Their stories of faith are similar. Gideon is named first in this verse. Gideon's story is found in Judges 6-8. The backdrop for Gideon, who was the fifth judge or deliverer of Israel, begins with the Israelites being ravaged by the Midianites as a consequence for their disobedience to God. The people finally cried out to God, and God heard their cries and graciously intervened by sending an angel to

Gideon to call him into leadership and service. Although Gideon was a willing servant of God, he needed some assurance, thus the fleece. Remember that? The event is found in Judges 6:36-40:

> So Gideon said to God, "If You will save Israel by my hand as You have said—look, I shall put a fleece of wool on the threshing floor; if there is dew on the fleece only, and it is dry on all the ground, then I shall know that You will save Israel by my hand, as You have said." And it was so. When he rose early the next morning and squeezed the fleece together, he wrung the dew out of the fleece, a bowlful of water. Then Gideon said to God, "Do not be angry with me, but let me speak just once more: Let me test, I pray, just once more with the fleece; let it now be dry only on the fleece, but on all the ground let there be dew." And God did so that night. It was dry on the fleece only, but there was dew on all the ground.

This was definitely a lapse for Gideon, but after getting the assurance that he needed, he proved himself to be a faithful and mighty warrior, as well as a strong leader of men. Gideon was far from perfect, but through faith he carried out God's mission by destroying the idols of Baal that his father and the community had been worshipping, and then by obeying God and leading three hundred men into battle against 135,000. They won the battle because they trusted the Lord to fight for them. True faith obeys God, it trusts God, it does God's will no matter how great the enemy and it boldly goes forward for the glory of God. Have faith like Gideon.

We might ask what that looks like in our lives today. How about this: obeying God when it's hard, doing the God-honoring thing even when there's going to be a price to be paid for doing it but still doing it, trusting God even when all kinds of enemies and obstacles are in front of us but still trusting and pursuing His glory in your life. Continuing on in Christ, exalting Christ and pleasing Christ even in great adversity. Faith.

Next is Barak. The account of Deborah and Barak is found in Judges 4 and 5, before Gideon. Because of Israel's sin, they had been under the control of the Canaanite king Jabin and the commander of his army, Sisera. The Canaanites had nine hundred chariots of iron and ruled over Israel for twenty years. Under God's authority, Deborah and Barak gathered ten-thousand troops and attacked Sisera and his army. That was done in great faith because there was no way they could win the battle in their own power. Instead, they had to go out in faith which they did, and God gave them a supernatural victory. The call? Faithfully obey God even when you stand against a great enemy. Trust God. Do the will of God no matter what and step out and leave the result to Him. Our call as Christians is clear: to trust and honor God no matter what. Sometimes He gives the victory and sometimes not, but the call remains the same. Faith understands this, and faith always steps forward and does the will of God.

Next is Samson, another judge. Samson was a worldly-minded man, but still God used him. Throughout his life Samson broke his vows to God. Samson had a lust problem, he was a womanizer and a vengeful man, and he's a terrible example for us in many ways. So why then is he listed here in Hebrews 11? The highlight of Samson's life is the way he finished.

In Judges 16, Samson has been captured by the Philistines, his eyes have been gouged out, and he has been brought into the Temple of Dagon to perform for the Philistines who wanted to mock him. Samson had his hands placed on the pillars of the Temple and then he prayed to the LORD, "O Sovereign LORD, remember me." That's a perfect prayer. He said, "O God, please strengthen me just once more, and let me with one blow get revenge on the Philistines for my two eyes." His great strength returned by the hand of God, he pushed against the pillars, the Temple fell, and everyone died.

I believe that at that moment Samson had truly repented and rested his hope fully on God. "Remember me, O Lord God." That's a prayer of renewal and repentance. It's a clear recognition of the source of his strength is in this prayer. With it, he prays to God in faith that God could forgive him, and then he pushes in faith, and the enemy is destroyed. And so, Samson died in faith, and that's a perfect example for us. Die well, die in faith, die trusting God and make your last breath one that is well pleasing to your creator. And then think about this: since we don't know when our time will come, the wise ones are those who are faithful today.

Every day is a gift. So live every day faithfully for God. Today might be your last day. Will you live faithfully for Him today? So die well and live well today. Or as the Apostle Paul put it in Ephesians 5:16, "Redeem the time because the days are evil." The idea is to buy up all the time we have and devote it to the Lord because these are serious times, and none of us knows how long we have left. Life is short, eternity is long, and we are to use the time that we have left to live faithfully for the glory of God. As Robert Murray M'Cheyne said, "Life is vanishing fast make haste for eternity."[97] As Spurgeon said, "Each time the clock ticks, death's footsteps are falling on the ground close behind you."[98] Or as J.C. Ryle said, "Years are slipping away, and time is flying. Graveyards are filling up and families are thinning. Death and judgment are getting nearer to us all. Awake before it's too late."[99]

There is no assurance of tomorrow and what we do for God is all that matters. Get in the radical flow of faithful living so that when your time comes—which may be soon—you have redeemed it for the glory of God.

---

[97] Andrew Bonar, *Memoir and Remains of Robert Murray M'Cheyne*, (Edinburg: Banner of Truth Trust, 1995), 27.
[98] Charles Spurgeon, "Watch-Night Service," Bible Bulletin Board, accessed 1/12/2022, https://www.biblebb.com/files/spurgeon/0059.HTM
[99] J.C. Ryle, *Holiness*, (Moscow, ID: Charles Nolan Publishers, 2002), 114.

Let's be like Samson and die well, but let's also live well today, faithfully honoring Him, battling sin fiercely and lifting Him high today.

Jephthah is mentioned next. Jephthah served as a judge over Israel for six years. His account is recorded in Judges 11 and 12. What about Jephthah stands out to us that is used as an example of what true faith in God looks like? In a word, Jephthah trusted the Lord. In faith he led the people into battle against a more powerful enemy, the Ammonites, and in faith they won the battle. So be like him in that aspect of faith. Obey God no matter what, even when you face opposition, and even when you may die. True faith is willing to obey God and it's willing to die obeying God, because pleasing Him to the death is more important than displeasing Him and remaining alive.

The encouragement? Be faithful to God in all things even when tragedy strikes, even when cancer hits, even when death comes or when pain abounds, stay faithful. Don't let anything cause you to take your eyes of faith off of the God who loves you. Trust Him, obey Him, be faithful to Him no matter what.

Faith says like Job, "Though He slay me, yet will I trust Him." Faith says, in agreement with William Cowper, "Judge not the Lord by feeble sense but trust Him for His grace. Behind a frowning providence He hides a smiling face."[100] Life is a battle, and our enemy is powerful, and our call is to go to war and fight well and leave the rest up to God. So, in faith we go out every day to fight well.

Next mentioned is David. Much is written about David in the Bible, and much could be said about David. He wasn't perfect, but he repented of his sin with Bathsheba, and he repented when he disobeyed God and took a census that he shouldn't have pridefully taken. The faithful repent

---

[100] William Cowper, "God Moves in a Mysterious Way", Hymnal.net, accesses 1/12/2022, https://www.hymnal.net/en/hymn/h/675

when they fail. David was indeed a man after God's heart, and even as a teenager, his great faith in the living God was put on display when he defeated Goliath. There's no way he should have defeated Goliath, but he trusted God and that changed everything.

This amazing event is recorded for us in 1Samuel 17. In verse 32, David said to King Saul, "Let no man's heart fail because of Goliath, your servant will go and fight with this Philistine." No one else would do it, but David went in faith in his God. Faith is bold. In verse 37 David said, "The Lord who delivered me from the paw of the lion and from the paw of the bear, He will deliver me from the hand of this Philistine." That's faith, but David didn't just say it, David acted on it and followed through. It begins in verse 45:

> Then David said to the Philistine, "You come to me with a sword, with a spear, and with a javelin. But I come to you in the name of the Lord of hosts, the God of the armies of Israel, whom you have defied. This day the Lord will deliver you into my hand, and I will strike you and take your head from you. And this day I will give the carcasses of the camp of the Philistines to the birds of the air and the wild beasts of the earth, that all the earth may know that there is a God in Israel. Then all this assembly shall know that the Lord does not save with sword and spear; for the battle is the Lord's, and He will give you into our hands.

That's real faith. Verse 48, "David hurried and ran toward the army to meet the Philistine." The next verse tells us that David slung a stone and it struck Goliath in the forehead, and the giant fell face down in the dirt. And then verse 51, "David ran and stood over the Philistine, took his sword and drew it out of its sheath and killed him, and cut off his head with it." And then the Philistines fled. This was all done in faith. Faith is bold, and faith acts out and trusts God with the result.

If you read the Psalms that David wrote, you see a man of great trials who always put his trust in God in the midst of those trials. The call is to have faith like David; to repent when you fail and return to God. We too are called to battle the giants who oppose God and his people, to be bold, to run to the battles at hand. We too must look to God in trials, to be men and women after God's heart like the faithful. We must always seek to glorify Him and to love Him with more fervor and passion. That's what faith does. Faith keeps seeking more, ever more of Him. It presses on in its love for God and his glory in your life. Have faith like David.

Next listed is Samuel. Samuel was an amazing man of God. He was a judge and a prophet of God, and in faith he led the children of Israel well. He was bold, he was fervent, he was zealous for the glory of God. He was uncompromising, and he spoke and lived the truth even when it could be very costly. Samuel faced a rebellious and idolatrous people and he faced them with courage and great conviction. He spoke God's Word. He thought nothing of personal protection and personal safety, but instead, God came first to Samuel. Samuel always said what he believed to be right against all threats. He was fearless because of his faith in the living God. We should seek to have faith like that. Be fearless and bold and uncompromising like Samuel. Don't make God just a part of your life—put Him first in your life and live like you believe it. Don't have a faith that treats God like a robot. Let it be real in your life. Let your life be compelled by your love of Him to do what you do, like Samuel. That's Biblical faith. That's true faith in the living God.

In Psalm 99:6, Samuel is cited alongside Moses and Aaron as men who called on God and were answered. Later in Israel's history, when the Israelites were living in disobedience to God, Jeremiah 15:1 tells us the Lord declared that they were beyond even the defense of Moses and

Samuel, two of Israel's greatest intercessors. This shows us what Samuel was like: a man of God, a man of prayer, a bold man, a faithful man. Like Samuel, faithful men pray much, they pray fervently. They get the attention of their watching God. They aren't fearful. They speak and live the truth. They have passion for God and His glory. They hate sin, they honor God with their lives, and they obey at all costs. Like Samuel.

Faith Principle 31
The prophets: The faithful put God first, above men and even death

Next mentioned are the prophets. With that, we sweep all the way from 1 Samuel down to the end of the Old Testament. The prophets were spokesmen for God, and their calling came with a very high price. Note that there are no more prophets today since we have the fully sufficient and completed written Word of God in our hands. But before that miracle came about, the prophets were the ones who spoke God's Word to the people. In faith they had to do this because they usually ended up dead. The call? To have faith like them, to put God first above men even if it means death, for God is worth it. Pleasing God is always worth it and the faithful understand this.

If you were called by God to be a prophet, you entered a life of suffering, pain and opposition. Take Jeremiah for example. God called Jeremiah to the ministry of prophet and Jeremiah's message was one of repentance. He went out and preached boldly and no one listened. It takes faith to preach to people like that. It gets worse because not only did the people refuse to listen, but the words Jeremiah spoke made the people extremely angry. In faith, he still preached; in faith he still obeyed God. Jeremiah has been called the weeping prophet and he lived a life of terrible conflict because of the unpopular message that he remained committed to in faith. Jeremiah was threatened, tried for his life, put in stocks, forced to flee from King Jehoiakim, publicly humiliated by a false prophet, thrown into prison, thrown down a well, taken to Egypt against his will, rejected by his family, rejected by his friends, rejected by his neighbors, rejected by his audience and rejected by the kings. In faith, Jeremiah stood alone. But God was with Him, and God was enough. Faith sees this, faith knows this and faith stays true to God no matter what. In Jeremiah 11:19, we see what he faced:

> But I was like a docile lamb brought to the slaughter, and I did not know that they had devised schemes against me saying, "Let us destroy the tree with its fruit, and let us cut him off from the land of the living, that his name may be remembered no more."

These people wanted to kill Jeremiah for preaching the truth in faith. In Jeremiah 15:15, he writes:

> O Lord You know; remember me and visit me and take vengeance for me on my persecutors. In Your enduring patience, do not take me away and know that for Your sake I have suffered rebuke... Why is my pain perpetual and my wound incurable, which refuses to be healed? Will you surely be to me like an unreliable stream, as waters that fail?

Because of his faith, Jeremiah is suffering. He is in pain, and he's feeling all alone and depressed. And so, he's praying for God to come and to help him. In Jeremiah 20:1, it just keeps getting worse.

> Now Pashur the son of Immer, the priest who was also the chief governor in the house of the Lord, heard that Jeremiah prophesied these things. Then Pashur struck Jeremiah the prophet and put him in the stocks that were in the high gate of Benjamin, which was by the house of the Lord.

So here he is taking physical punishment for his faithfulness to God and to his calling. It continues in Jeremiah 26:8 and 9:

> Now it happened that when Jeremiah had made an end of speaking all that the Lord had commanded him to speak to all the people, that the priests and the prophets and all the people seized him, saying, "You will surely die!" … And all the people were gathered together against Jeremiah in the house of the Lord.

Jeremiah's pain for preaching God's truth continued. Jeremiah 37:15 says, "Therefore the princes were angry with Jeremiah, and they struck him and put him in prison." Then, Jeremiah 38:6, "So they took Jeremiah and cast him into the dungeon of Malkiah the king's son, which was in the court of the prison, and they let Jeremiah down with ropes. And in the dungeon there was no water but mire. So Jeremiah sank in the mire." In chapter 40, Jeremiah is taken away in chains, and later we read how he was again rejected by the people. All of this and more because of his faith. But in faith he still preached. In faith he still obeyed.

We find that God didn't permit Jeremiah to marry as an illustration to the people of Judah. There is no indication that he ever had any followers—none who really heard and heeded his message. Can you imagine how a conversation between God and Jeremiah might have gone?

"Hey Jeremiah. I want you to preach for me. I want you to speak my words to my people. What do you say?"

"Sounds great, God. Can't wait!"

"Oh, by the way Jeremiah, just a few things first: you can't marry, you will suffer terribly, you will weep often, you won't have any followers, the people will hate and reject you and no one's going to listen to you."

And amazingly in faith, Jeremiah shrugs and says, "Okay Lord."

That's Jeremiah. The example is to have faith like Jeremiah and the prophets who suffered such rejection. Put God first no matter what. Look ahead, obey at all costs, look to the reward, never give in. Don't compromise, don't quit, don't stop fighting, never slow down until you are in glory. The faithful battle on.

In early 16th century Great Britain, a traditional English folk song, *Sir Andrew Barton*, describes the final battle of this Scottish privateer who gained notoriety by his raids against Portuguese ships. Verses cite a wounded Barton encouraging his men. "Fight on, my men. A little I'm hurt but not yet slain. I'll just lie down and bleed a while, and then I'll rise and fight again."[101]

The faithful rise and keep battling. Some say Jeremiah died from being stoned to death, but so be it. Faith says God is worth every bit of it. Faith doesn't care what happens to your mortal body here, faith cares about pleasing God with the one short life you have knowing that glory awaits. Have faith like the prophets, that's the encouragement.

---

[101] Thomas Moore, Good Reads, accessed 1/12/2022, https://www.goodreads.com/quotes/774409-fight-on-my-men-says-sir-andrew-barton-i-am-hurt-but

Faith Principle 32
The faithful live for the next life

Verses 33-35 in Hebrews 11 tell us a little more about what true faith looks like:

> ...who through faith subdued kingdoms, worked righteousness, obtained promises, stopped the mouths of lions, quenched the violence of fire, escaped the edge of the sword, out of weakness were made strong, became valiant in battle, turned to flight the armies of the aliens. Women received their dead raised to life again. Others were tortured, not accepting deliverance, that they might obtain a better resurrection.

Here we continue to learn about true faith. True faith overcomes great obstacles, and our call is to trust and obey Him and leave the rest up to Him. That's what the prophets and the others did, and God was well pleased. Look what it says. They subdued, overcame, over-powered and overthrew kingdoms. That's exactly what Gideon, Barak, Samson, Jephthah and David did in faith. They obeyed and trusted God, and God moved according to His will.

They also worked righteousness. In other words, in faith they lived for the glory of God; rightly, correctly and biblically. Even though it was very difficult, they did it anyway because in faith they looked to God. And in faith they knew that pleasing God was the best in the eternal scheme— even though it means some suffering for now. Faith looks ahead and obeys.

These were men who did what was right no matter the cost. How is that possible? Doing what's right and Godly even though it costs you your friends. Doing what's right and Godly even though it costs you your job. Doing what's right and Godly even though it costs you your status in the eyes of the people. Doing what's right and Godly even though it brings you great physical pain and torment. Doing what's right and Godly even though it means you will go to prison. Doing what's right and Godly even though it costs you your life. How is that possible? Faith.

In faith, I can say, "I believe in God; I know what the future holds. I know that obeying God has eternal value. I know that this life is fading and fleeting, and in faith I know that obeying God is always worth it." This is faith, and faith allows such a response. "I won't compromise even though refusing to compromise brings me great pain. Pleasing God is worth the pain." Faith.

In faith these men also obtained promises. This is talking about the promises of God to these people. They trusted what God had promised, and those promises were realized. Promises of victory as experienced by Joshua, Gideon, Barak and David. Note what it says back in Hebrews 6:13:

> For when God made the promise to Abraham, since He could swear by no one greater, He swore by Himself, saying, *"I will surely bless you and I will surely multiply you."* And so, having patiently waited, he obtained the promise.

There you see it happening with Abraham. So many of the faithful of the past lived out their faith and they patiently trusted in the Lord and His promises. Many of them saw those promises realized with their physical eyes. In faith.

But then look down to verse 39, "And all these having obtained good testimony through faith, did not receive the promise." So here, they did not all receive the promise even though they had great faith. When you put your trust in God and live faithfully for Him you will see many great things happen in this life, where you are just amazed at God. These are things like the money came in, the child was healed, the loved one was saved, the perfect job was found and so on. But also, you might not. What then? You keep trusting.

Every promise God has made to you will indeed come to pass as His beloved child, but most of those promises won't be fully realized until we arrive in glory. Until then we keep trusting, obeying and pressing ahead in faith. It takes greater faith to stand true to God when the heavens seem silent to our prayers than when He is answering in great victories. Regardless, the call is to stay faithful. God keeps all His promises—if not in this life, then always in the next. And the next is much better. Your call is to walk in faith through the blessings and through the fires.

What else? Through faith they stopped the mouths of lions. This was Daniel. In faith Daniel went into the lions' den believing God would take care of him. And so, God shut the mouths of the lions. Also in faith, Daniel accepted that it was also okay if the lions' mouths weren't shut and he was to be eaten. God can be trusted with all of that. True faith stays faithful.

In faith the violence of the fire was quenched. This refers to Daniel's three friends, Shadrach, Meshach and Abednego. In faith they stood up for the Lord against everyone, refusing to bow down to Nebuchadnezzar while knowing they would be thrown into the fire. In faith they went into the fire, and they didn't get burned.

Remember what they said? "We're not going to bow down to you. And if we go in the fire, we'll burn. Or maybe we won't burn. But in any case, we will not bow down to you." That's real faith. Either way, they trusted the Lord, and this time they didn't get burned. Note that many throughout history had great faith like that and yet were burned to death. Still, faith trusts God through it all, for God knows what's best. Our call is to trust Him and obey regardless. For this is what faith in the God who saved your soul does. "Maybe God will rescue me from this fire. Maybe

I'll get burned really bad. Maybe I'll burn to death. So be it, for I trust God with all of that, and my call is to walk by faith and leave the rest up to Him."

In faith they also escaped the edge of the sword. That was true of David. No matter how often Saul tried to kill David by pinning him to the wall with his sword or by chasing him around the country, he never could do it. God was with David, and in faith David sought God's glory in his life. Faith doesn't compromise even when people want to seek your death.

The writer of Hebrews also said: "Out of weakness they were made strong." We are all weak, but in faith we are strong. Faith requires recognizing our weakness but at the same time, laying hold of God's strength. Where's your faith? These weak men did great things for God through faith. "In faith they became valiant in battle and turned to fight the armies of the aliens, and women received their dead raised to life again." That happened in 1 Kings 17. That's where Elijah healed the dead son of the widow of Zarephath. In 2 Kings 4, Elisha raised the child of the Shunammite woman from the dead. In faith. They trusted God and God did great and amazing things.

I'm convinced that the church is so weak today because we have so little faith in the God of all creation. Where are the bold men and women of God these days? Where are the men and women like Daniel, and like Shadrach, Meshach and Abednego? Where are the Elijah's? Where are the Jeremiah's? True faith can conquer anything because our faith is in God. Unless of course God chooses not to let His people conquer, but rather, He chooses to refine them through the struggle. Even still, we trust Him with it all.

What's the call? To trust God and to live out our faith with boldness, passion and fervor, knowing that God will either pull us out of it, or walk us through it according to His will. Again, our call is to trust Him and to boldly obey Him no matter what. The weak in faith give in to peer pressure and temptation, they choose mediocrity over radical faith in the living God. They choose ease over redeeming the time. They are passionless and earthly minded. Not so us.

As British missionary to India William Carey said, "Expect great things from God; attempt great things for God."[102] Where is the expecting and where is the attempting in you? Note that this gets down to the very nitty gritty of life; faithful living. So how are you faring in your battle against sin? The faithful fight it and they never give in. Have you applied your faith to your daily job or routine so that you reflect God's righteousness by your integrity and honesty? Do you live like heaven is your real home? How does it show? Where's your faith? Hebrews 11 faith trusts God, fights on the front lines of the spiritual battle, hates sin and loves holiness, pursues God's glory and keeps on until his or her dying breath. Lord helps us to have a faith like that.

Without skipping a beat, the author continues with the second part of verse 35, "... and others were tortured, not accepting their release, so that they might obtain a better resurrection." Now the tune has changed. We were just talking about faith overcoming great obstacles in verses 32-35, but now the writer talks about being tortured for the faith and not being rescued from it. And then from there it only seems to get worse. And so, after reading the first part of the list, you might think, "These guys on the second half of the list must not have had faith." But that's not true because the author continues in verse 39, "And all these, having obtained a good testimony through faith." This changes things. This means that the truly faithful may indeed be delivered from their struggle or not, and many of the faithful were not. And like them, you may not be delivered out of your struggle either, even if your faith is great.

---

[102] S. Pearce Carey, *William Carey*, (London: The Wakeman Trust, 1993), 77.

That said, those on the second half of the list were people of faith, just as much as those on the first half. In fact, you could argue that they had greater faith because it's not as easy to trust God when you're being scourged, stoned or sawn in two, as it is when you're seeing foreign armies put to flight and the dead raised to life. And while we would all sign up to be in the first group, we need to recognize that sometimes—if not many times—God is pleased to withhold spectacular results, and bless us instead with His grace as our sufficiency in overwhelming trials. That's not pleasant but it greatly honors the Lord. The call is to trust Him and obey Him through it all.

Sometimes you might even need to endure torture for Christ because of your faith, and the call is to endure faithfully. The word for torture is from the Greek word *tumpanon*, from which we get our English word tambourine.[103] The word means to stretch a person on an instrument of torture resembling a drum and then to beat that person with clubs usually to death. This was a horrible and painful way to die. And here we find that God's faithful are willing to be beaten to death rather than compromise their faith in Him. They are willing to face torture rather than dishonor their Lord. In faith, they aren't willing to sacrifice their future in eternity on an altar of the immediate. Therefore, they walked into being tortured, not accepting deliverance, that they might obtain a better resurrection.

Not accepting deliverance means they weren't willing to compromise their faith to get out of the torturing.[104] They weren't willing to denounce Christ or their faith to make things easier on themselves. Deliverance was offered to them, but only at the price of turning away from the Lord. They had a choice: a choice to be disloyal to Christ or endure the most excruciating suffering; surrender the truth or be tortured by devils in

---

[103] Vine, 145.
[104] Wuest, Vol. 10, 209.

human form. If you were disloyal to Christ, if you surrendered the truth then you could be free from this horrible torture. The faithful say, "No, give me the torture. He died for me, I must remain true and loyal to Him." So, the faithful esteem the eternal interest of their soul and the Lord Himself over the present comfort of their physical bodies. Note that they were no better than we are, for they were people just like us. But they trusted Christ with their lives and with their circumstances. Love should compel you to remain true to Him who died on a cross in your place. What do you esteem more highly, your body or your soul? The faithful know what's most valuable in the little things of life, day in and day out, and also when the torture comes.

These faithful ones stayed true to God even though it meant pain and torture. They still stayed faithful. "Jesus is Lord."

As the torturing got worse. "Jesus is Lord!"

As the beatings grew more intense. "Jesus is Lord!"

Coming from their torturer, they heard, "If you just say Jesus isn't Lord, I'll stop, and your pain will end. I'll even let you go free."

"Jesus is Lord, I'll never deny Him, Jesus is Lord!"

Have faith like that, for certainly your God is worth it. We are called to emulate their faith.

The verse continues on to say that these faithful men sought a better resurrection. This could mean a couple of different things. First, it could mean that because of their faithfulness in life, and because they lived for that which has eternal value and that reaps eternal reward, that when they die and see the Lord, that their resurrection will result in a greater blessing and reward than if they had avoided suffering. How we live out our faith matters, and when you honor God with your life and bear fruit for His glory, it reaps eternal reward. Certainly dying for the faith has eternal value that will be rewarded by God accordingly. "Well done my good and faithful servant." This is true.

It could also mean this: the beginning of verse 35 mentioned women receiving their dead back to life again. And so, in context, this could refer to a resurrection which is better than the temporary resurrections just alluded to because those people were revived only to die again. But believers receive a resurrection which is "permanent," and from which they will never die again. So those who were tortured for their faith in the Lord were eagerly looking forward to what lay ahead for them the other side of death. The earthly results of faith are unpredictable, but the heavenly results are certain. And what faith wants most isn't the earthly victories but the heavenly home, the enduring hope that sustains someone even if his faith leads him into earthly suffering. And this is what I think the writer is alluding to, for it fits within the context of this passage.

For a mother to have her dead child returned to her is about the best thing anyone could ever hope for on this earth. And yet, the writer considers that something "better" happened to those who were tortured, for they obtained a far better resurrection than those children. They awakened in glory, in eternal glory. John Piper says it like this:

> The common feature of the faith that escapes suffering and the faith that endures suffering is this: Both of them involve believing that God Himself is better than what life can give to you now—and better than what death can take from you later. When you can have it all, faith says that God is better; and when lose it all, faith says that God is better. ... What does faith believe in the moment of torture? That if God loved me, He would get me out of this? No. Faith believes that there is a kind of resurrection for believers which is better than the miracle of escape. Way better than the

> kind of resurrection experienced by the widow's son, who returned to life only to die again later.[105]

If I am tortured and die for the Lord, I will awaken with Him, and what's better than that? This should encourage us to endure rejection, ill-treatment, injustice, and if need be even torture and death for the sake of the gospel. He's worth it all, for again, the better resurrection awaits us in glory.

In 155 A.D., Polycarp the Bishop of Smyrna was sentenced to die, to burn at the stake for being a Christian who lived and preached the truth of God.[106] He was 86 years old when they burned him to death. When ordered to recant and say that Caesar is God, he replied, "Eighty-six years I have served Him, and He has done me no wrong. How can I blaspheme my King who saved me?"

To his persecutors, he said, "You threaten me with the fire that burns for a time and is quickly quenched, but you do not know the fire which awaits the wicked in the judgment to come and in everlasting punishment. Why are you waiting? Come and do what you will." And he died for the Lord, and he is reaping his eternal reward. More than 1,800 years in heaven, the better resurrection. It's well worth it.

John Rodgers was also a preacher during the reign of Bloody Mary.[107] He was strong, bold, courageous and he feared God more than he feared man. He was sentenced to prison for preaching the Word, and later sentenced to death. Reports say that he awaited death cheerfully, even

---

[105] John Piper, "Faith to Be Strong and Faith to Be Weak," Desiring God, accesses 1/12/2022, https://www.desiringgod.org/messages/faith-to-be-strong-and-faith-to-be-weak

[106] John Foxe, *Foxe's Book of Martyrs*, (Peabody, MA: Hendrickson Publishers, 2004), 14.

[107] Ibid, 267.

though he was forbidden to say goodbye to his own wife. He was told he could recant and go home but he refused. He said, "That which I have preached I will seal with my blood." He was called a heretic. Rodgers replied, "That shall be known at the Day of Judgment." His executioner said, "I will never pray for you." Rodgers replied, "Ah, but I shall pray for you." It was said that he was burnt to ashes, and as he burned, witnesses saw him washing his hands in the flames. Rodgers has been in heaven for more than 450 years; the better resurrection because it was well worth it. Some things are worth dying for. Dying for Christ is always better than living for man. The faithful know this and they live accordingly.

Perhaps you say, "I will never see the day when I will have to be tortured or martyred for my faith so I'm safe." Wrong. For this is a day-by-day thing, a thing that permeates every aspect of your life. Jesus gives us the principle mentioned here in Mark 8:34, "Whoever desires to come after me, let him deny himself, and take up his cross, and follow me." This means that every day we are faithful to the Lord, every day we put Jesus first, every day we say no to self and yes to Him, and every day He is Lord in the little things and also in the big things. And then if they come to torture me, my mind has already been made up: "Him. I am faithful to Him. Not me, not you, not anything else, Him. So, come on and torture me, He's worth it. He will help me. He will never forsake me. Come on, I've been ready for this for a long time. Him!" Faith gives us this heavenly and eternal mindset.

CHAPTER 16

Mount Whitney Trail 2014:

Oh no, no, no. I knew immediately that I had just broken my foot. Over the years, I have broken numerous bones in my body, but this was different because I was still on the trail on Mount Whitney.

Remember, Mount Whitney is the highest mountain in the contiguous United States at 14,505 feet elevation.[108] From the east, the trail to the top is eleven miles with an elevation gain of 6,960 feet. In other words, the hike, up and back, is brutal. Many people do it over a two or even a three-day period, but some do the whole twenty-two miles in one day. Due to time constraints, I had only a day to hike. So, I awoke at 1 a.m., quickly got ready and had my dad drive me up to the Whitney Portal Campground where the trail began. He dropped me off in the dark and I began my hike while my dad drove back down to our room in Lone Pine and

---

[108] Wenk, 1.

went back to sleep. I had hiked the trail before a couple of times but at this point, I'd never hiked it alone. I wasn't worried. On this trail you are never really alone as people are scattered all over the trail, either day hiking it like me, or making it a multi-day excursion. That said, I loved the opportunity to be relatively alone. I like the solitude. It's a great opportunity to pray and to get refocused. The stars above were amazing and I felt I was in my element. I hiked, I prayed, I even sang a little and I thought about the Lord and my own spiritual life. I was enjoying God's creation as I huffed and puffed along.

The sun was beginning to come up as I arrived at the dreaded ninety-nine switchbacks about seven miles into the hike. They take you back and forth up the side of a mountain that is adjacent to Whitney, going from just over 12,000 feet to 13,700 feet. Those two miles are slow and painful as you really begin to feel the elevation. This is where the headaches begin along with the nausea. The last two miles aren't nearly as hard as the switchbacks, but the trail is rougher, and the elevation makes for slow progress.

I finally made it to the top and the view was outstanding. I signed a logbook that awaits all hikers who make it. I took my time to rest. I took some pictures, ate a little of the snacks that I'd packed and then loaded my backpack and headed back down the way I came. Coming down is much easier on the lungs, but it can also be described as extremely mundane as it seems to take forever. The trail is rocky and uneven, so you need to be careful and watchful about every step you take. After a while, all you want to do is get to the end, eat a hamburger at the portal restaurant, take a shower and then go to bed. It's easy to allow your mind to wander. Everything was going well and I was about a mile and a half from the end of the trail when it happened. I had let my guard down and I carelessly stepped on an uneven rock that had some dust on it that caused my foot to slip and bang against another rock. Just like that my foot was broken. I actually felt it give way, and in my head I heard the snap. That little bone on the far side of the foot had just broken into two. Now what? I shifted the weight to take the pressure off my foot. The pain actually wasn't that bad, yet. It hurt, but it wasn't a horrible pain. I took a tentative step. Crunch. I could literally feel the bones rubbing together. But again, the pain wasn't terrible. I started thinking about how I was going to handle this. I thought if I was careful, if I walked really slow and if I shifted all my weight onto the inside of my foot, I might make it down. I used my walking stick much more than I had before and I found that if I leaned on it, I could actually move forward. What other choice did I have? There was no way I was going to call for a rescue squad to come and carry me down the trail. I don't know what something like a rescue squad costs, but I know I'm way too cheap for it. I told myself I had a choice: either walk out or crawl out. I began to walk carefully, slowly and painfully.

The rocky gradient going down the trail was treacherous to navigate. About every third step something would go wrong, and it would send pain shooting through my foot. A creek crossing that had been without incident on my way up the trail turned brutal coming down. To reach the other side you had to maintain your balance as you glide from rock to rock over the water, and there was only room for one foot on each rock. This forced me to bear down my full weight on the broken foot repeatedly to get across the creek. It was rough. After the creek, crossing the trail became easier to navigate. Again, it was painful, but not impossible. Step, step, crunch. Step, step, crunch.

With about a half a mile left I saw my dad coming up the trail to meet me. I called out, "Dad, I broke my foot!"

"Hold up son, while I take your picture."

He hadn't heard me. The moment was bizarre, the request so surreal that I almost laughed. So I posed for a picture. Click. He came closer. I tried again. "Dad, I broke my foot." This time I wasn't sure he believed it was actually broken. We slowly made our way down to the portal, which marked the end of the trail. The closer I got, the more painful my foot felt inside my boot. The adrenaline was wearing off and what had started as a slow pace deteriorated into a hobble as we finally made it to the end. My dad wanted to head directly to the car, but I pointed in the general direction of the prize that I'd been longing for the whole hike. We ate a hamburger at the small restaurant that caters to the hikers and campers who stay there. Then we went to the hospital where I had X-rays taken (yes it was broken) and they put me in a temporary splint until the swelling went down and I could later get a proper cast.

This is what faithfulness in the Christian life sometimes looks like. It keeps going even in the midst of great pain. It means continuing on no matter what because all the other options aren't options for you.

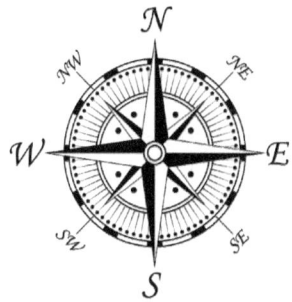

Faith Principle 33
The faithful endure

Verses 36-40, the writer of Hebrews continues to tell us about true faith.

> Still others had trial of mockings and scourgings, yes, and of chains and imprisonment. They were stoned, they were sawn in two, were tempted, were slain with the sword. They wandered about in sheepskins and goatskins, being destitute, afflicted, tormented—of whom the world was not worthy. They wandered in deserts and mountains, in dens and caves of the earth. And all these, having obtained a good testimony through faith, did not receive the promise, God having provided something better for us, that they should not be made perfect apart from us.

Here we see that in faith, these faithful greats in the past endured to the end for Christ. They stayed faithful. They chose it; they walked into it for Christ. The phrase, trial of mockings, involves public ridicule, of people scoffing, calling out derisive remarks.[109] And while we might all agree that mocking is better than the torture rack, it's still not pleasant. In fact, this area of suffering for our faith is very painful to our soul,

---

[109] Kittel, vol. 5, 625–626.

especially so when it comes from those whom we love. The faithful endure this and they remain faithful.

Other faithful ones were scourged. This involves being whipped in a manner designed to inflict the greatest amount of pain and torture upon the victim's flesh. This punishment was one of the things the Roman soldiers did to Jesus Himself. Other faithful ones have faced chains and imprisonment because of their faith in Christ; because of their allegiance to Christ. They were thrown into prison and chained because they were faithful to the Lord.

Others were stoned. Stephen in Acts is an example along with others. In 2 Chronicles 24:20, a priest by the name of Zechariah, a faithful man of God, spoke up for the Lord in the midst of a rebellious people. He said, "Why do you transgress the commandment of the Lord so that you cannot prosper? Because you have forsaken the Lord, He has forsaken you."

The response of the crowd? "At the command of the king they stoned him with stones in the court of the house of the Lord." Think of that. Being stoned to death for your faith. This is brutal, gruesome. The faithful endure this type of treatment if it comes, for the Lord. He's worth it to them. For they look ahead, and they love the Lord more than getting relief from the pain.

Others were sawn in two for their faith. Who is the writer talking about? Tradition says that the wicked King Manasseh killed the prophet Isaiah by sawing him in two with a wooden saw.[110] The faithful endure this for they love Him, and they look ahead.

Others were tempted. The belief is this refers to the many temptations that were offered to these faithful ones to recant and turn. Can you

---

[110] G.W. Bromily, *The International Standard Bible Encyclopedia*, vol. 2, (Grand Rapids, MI: Eerdman's Publishing Co, 1982), 886.

imagine what the one who sought to undermine their faith might have said? "If you recant then not only will you escape a painful death, but you'll be able to see your dying child. Just deny Christ and your pain will end. Just turn on the Lord and you and your family will be safe." Yet, they remained faithful, and they trusted God with the rest. Do you trust Him or not? Do you really believe that you are under His care? The faithful believe it, they live like it—and they die like it. Be like them.

Others were slain with the sword. That sounds like an absolutely horrible way to die. The word for sword here refers to a relatively short weapon like a dagger. Many of God's people were put to death for their faith by daggers like this. But Christ was worth it to them.

What else? "They wandered about in sheepskins and goatskins, being destitute, afflicted, tormented of whom the world was not worthy. They wandered in deserts and mountains, in dens and caves of the earth." Think of what these people had given up for the cause of the Lord? Why would they wander about in sheepskins and goatskins? The simple answer is that these were the only clothing that they had to wear. They were destitute because of their faith. The word for *destitute* means to fail in something, to come short of, to miss and to not reach.[111] And here it's talking about those who are lacking, about those who have to go without. The picture? That because of their faithfulness they lose their jobs, their livelihood, their source of income, their houses, any source of comfort they might have had. They've lost everything, and literally all they have left is the Lord. But in faith they choose nothing and Christ over everything without Christ, knowing that He is worth it.

They were also *afflicted*. The word literally means to press, to squeeze and to crush. It can refer to both physical suffering as well as emotional

---

[111] Vine, 302.

and spiritual suffering and affliction[112]. They were *tormented*, which means to be ill-treated, mistreated, harassed and oppressed.[113] This word is used in the present tense which indicates that these faithful ones were continually harassed. These faithful ones literally lost everything for the cause of the Lord. But they still remained faithful. How? Faith. They knew He is worth it. They knew the end is worth it when they were going to stand in glory.

They also "wandered in deserts and mountains, in dens and caves of the earth." Why? Because of their faith in God. They had no homes, they had to flee. They had to wander, to find whatever means they could to stay alive. Was it worth it? Without a doubt, for God it's always worth it.

How are all these things possible? Faith. They looked ahead, they knew, they trusted God. They knew that nothing in this life is worth what awaits them in the next life. The call is to have faith like that.

Faith Principle 34
The faithful greatly please God

I love how the writer of Hebrews describes these faithful people: they were people of whom the world was not worthy. The basic thought with this statement is that these people were a gift to the world, a gift from God to this dark and evil world that did not merit them. They were more fit for heaven than they were fit for this fallen place. They stood out and proclaimed, "The Lord is better than life so turn and believe and be saved; live for Him no matter what because He's worth it all." And in faith they shined forth in the midst of this crooked and depraved generation.

"Of whom the world was not worthy" expresses the divine estimate. This is what God thinks of these people. See, the world was too evil to see

---

[112] Ibid, 38.
[113] Ibid, 144.

the worth of these faithful ones. But God sees, and God is well pleased. What else matters? The world deemed them unworthy to live, unworthy to be comfortable, unworthy to be affirmed or approved. The world felt diminished by their presence. But the reality is that the world was not worthy of them. The world didn't deserve them for they were so otherworldly, so heavenly minded, so Christlike. God was well pleased.

The writer goes on to give one great promise: that the faithful obtain a good testimony. This takes us all the way back to the second verse of chapter 11. "For by it, by faith the elders obtained a good testimony." And this is what faith does. Remember, the word *testimony* means to receive praise or approval.[114] So this means they lived by faith and therefore God approved of them. What could be better than that? The world didn't approve, the world wasn't worthy of them, but that doesn't matter because God Almighty approved of them. Because of their faith that was lived out. And so, God bore witness to these faithful ones in the victory of their faith over all obstacles. They trusted God and God was pleased. This is the kind of faith God commends. So here is the truth: God approves of those who operate on faith, who live out their faith as described here in Hebrews 11.

Hebrews 11 shows us that clear fact: Abel believed God and he sacrificed to God by faith and God approved of his sacrifice. Enoch believed God that he wouldn't die, and he didn't so God was pleased, and God approved. Noah believed God that it would rain, and he inherited righteousness for believing God, and God approved. Abraham and Sarah believed God for a child, and God approved of their faith, and they received a child. Fourteen people listed in chapter 11—Isaac, Jacob, Joseph, the parents of Moses, Moses, Joshua, Rahab, Gideon, Barak, Samson, Jephthah, David and Samuel—all believed God, and God said, "I

---

[114] Kittel, vol. 4, p. 474.

approve." They trusted in what they couldn't see. They lived their lives for the glory of God, and because of their faith God said, "Oh that's good, I approve." The world often ridicules or despises the person who lives by faith, but so what so long as God approves?

Note that the end of verse 39 says, "all these did not receive the promise." What does that mean? "All these," refers to all who have been mentioned in this chapter, which includes those who overcame great obstacles by faith, and those who had to endure great trials by faith. They all obtained a good testimony through their faith, yet none received the promise. It's important to note the singular nature of promise. In their earthly lives, each of them obtained many promises from God. But none of them obtained the promise. So, what's the promise?

The answer is Christ and what He gives us in the New Covenant. Those listed in Hebrews 11 all saw Him from afar, in types and shadows. But we see Him clearly, revealed in the New Testament. We clearly see this side of the cross, we understand who Jesus is and what He did when He shed His blood and died on that cross in our place. And while the Old was good, it could only point forward to that which is better, Jesus. And while the Old Testament saints were saved by grace through faith, their sin wasn't truly paid for in full until Christ came and died in their place on the cross as their sin was placed onto Him. He bled and died as their sacrifice and substitute, something that the Old always pointed towards. But now in Christ the reality has come, and we today see that clearly.

The author's point in saying this is simple. If the Old Testament saints were so faithful through all their trials even though they only saw things dimly and never received the fulfilled promise of Christ in the flesh, how much more should we be faithful? We understand things clearly and we have Christ. At the very least we should live out our faith in equal measure to theirs. In fact, we should be able to live out our faith in greater measure today. We have the better, Jesus, and this should affect the way we live. It should compel us forward in our faithfulness in this fading and fleeting life.

Such an interesting phrase, "that they should not be made perfect apart from us." While *perfect* means to be made complete, we should make note of two thoughts regarding the context.[115] First, no one was made perfect or complete until Christ came and died on the cross. Again, believers in the Old Testament were saved, but not until Jesus' work on the cross was complete and sin paid for in full could salvation be perfect. So the phrase "apart from us" shows how every believer in history is made perfect—through Christ. They looked forward to what Christ would do in faith, and we look back at what Christ has done in faith. We are all in this together under Christ and His work on the cross.

But also note the full realization of all God's promises won't be realized until we arrive in glory. And although we have the promise of Christ, we don't yet have the full experience of the glory that will be revealed with Him in heaven. And so, we must, like the Old Testament saints, live by faith in God's promise until He comes for us or until we go to Him in glory. The something better obviously is Christ. While it is centered on what He did in our place on the cross, it will be fully realized in the future in eternal glory. This is something the faithful ones eagerly look forward to, and it's something they live in light of.

As the faithful, we are indeed seeking a better country, that is, a heavenly one. And we live like we believe it, for our homeland isn't here. A heavenly country awaits us, the city of God awaits us, the city which has foundations whose builder and maker is God. He awaits the faithful. And this reality propels us on in our faith.

Soon we will arrive, but until then we walk by faith—passionate, loving, confident and expectant faith. Faith is ready to sacrifice present

---

[115] Kittel, vol. 8, 49.

comfort for future reward with Christ. Faith recognizes that this life is very short in comparison to eternity. Faith lives not with a focus on people or things, but with a God-ward focus. Faith looks not to this vapor of life but to eternity. Faith trusts and obeys God, leaving the results to His sovereignty.

Faithfulness to Jesus Christ counts more than anything else, more even than life itself. Why care if you are beaten for your faith when heaven awaits. Why care if you have to suffer here when heaven awaits. Why care if this life is filled with pain and trial and struggle when heaven awaits. Why care about the fading gifts of this fleeting life, He is waiting for you. And the wise ones are those who live out their faith radically, with passion, with fervor and without compromise, for soon you will be home. He's worth it. Lord help us to live faithfully today. Don't you eagerly long for God to say to you one day: "I approve, I am well pleased?" May it be so for us, as we faithfully live for the glory of God in this brief and fading life.

CONCLUSION

John Muir Trail:

Our next to the last day on the trail was going to be a tough one. We camped looking up at Mount Whitney. We were ahead of schedule, so even though we could have finished the hike on the fourteenth day, we still had one more night on the trail since our friends were picking us up at the trailhead in two days. The good news about this is we could get to the portal early in the morning to have one of their massive pancakes on top of the other full breakfast we were planning on eating.

It was amazing to have come this far. More than two-hundred miles, filled with peaks and valleys, hardships, hunger, pains and setbacks. Additionally, there were some incredible beauty, great prayer times, new friends and some good fellowship with Dave. That morning, we got up at 4:30 a.m., packed up, ate and headed up, way up. This was my first time hiking the west side up Mount Whitney and doing it with a full pack was tough. When we reached the end of the John Muir Trail, we dropped our backpacks, grabbed a water bottle and some food, and headed up the final two miles to the top of Mount Whitney. What a relief. I must say, we were pretty proud of ourselves to have finished the hike. It felt great, even though we still had eleven miles to go down the other side of the Mount Whitney trail. We ate, took pictures, signed the logbook and then headed back to where we had dropped our packs. Since we were early, we hiked six more miles and made our camp for the night.

The next morning, we traveled the three miles left to the portal and we sat down to the best breakfast we have ever had. It was amazing, a huge pancake covered with melted butter and rich syrup. We couldn't finish it, but we sure tried. We nearly made ourselves sick from eating too much, but it was worth it. Finishing the John Muir Trail felt like a great accomplishment. Completing something that hard was very rewarding. A bonus at the end was the meal we shared. Somehow, good food turns into excellent food when you're hungry. How much more the Christian life? We are all on a pilgrimage to home and the call is to walk faithfully, and to walk well all the way to the end. No quitting. The reward is truly remarkable: we will have our beloved Lord to welcome us along with an eternal feast of unending joy. Walk well, walk faithfully, walk to the end, no quitting.

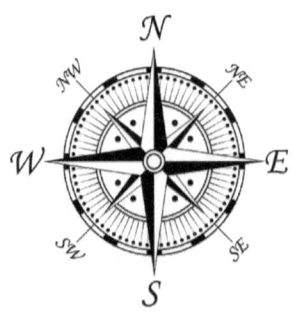

The greatest thing in life is glorifying and pleasing the God whom you love. Our God is certainly worthy of giving our all to, and the Christian's greatest joy comes in honoring Him with a faithful life. Like the elders of old, I want to obtain a good testimony from God. Like the faithful in Hebrews 11, I want it said of me: "God is not ashamed to be called their God." Like the faithful men and women of the past, I want it to be said of me, "Of whom the world was not worthy." Faithfulness is the key. The writer of Hebrews offers encouragement and, at the same time, a great challenge: pursue faithfulness and commit yourself to the qualities of faithfulness that have been shown to us in Hebrews 11. This pleases God and has value for all eternity.

God saved us by His amazing and undeserved grace. We don't deserve forgiveness and life, but we get it in overflowing abundance by grace through faith in Christ as Lord and Savior. What else matters in light of this? As the saved, we now faithfully live it out in growing measure. It begins by first trusting in God as Creator, knowing that we are not our own, but we belong to Him, and we will answer to Him. He is the fountainhead of all things, and our greatest joy and purpose comes when we give ourselves over to Him freely and without reservation from a heart of love. The faithful love God from the heart so that they are compelled by that love to please God with their fading lives. They seek Him first, and they are moved less and less by the things of this world. As they grow, Christ grows bigger and everything else grows smaller. This is true for the faithful ones.

The faithful are those who fear God. As they grow, they see themselves and their sin more clearly. They also see God and His majesty and holiness more clearly, and they respond in fearful reverence for Him. This fear drives them to seek to obey Him and to exalt Him more in their lives. The thought that, "He alone is worthy, and I am not. Therefore, I will lift Him high." This fear also compels the faithful to trust Him and to take Him at His Word, even when it doesn't seem to make sense from a worldly perspective. Faith sees through our sinful perspective and believes and obeys God. Reverential fear for God compels the faithful ones to trust Him even if no one else will. The faithful ones step out and trust God. This usually comes with a price. Sometimes it means ridicule, and sometimes it means pain and death. But God is worth it. The faithful ones don't live for the here and now, they live for God's glory and for what lies ahead. God is faithful, and the faithful ones don't let what they can see and understand from a human perspective cause them to veer from trusting and obeying Him.

God alone is our rock, and the faithful ones are anchored to their only rock. Storms won't cause the faithful ones to cut the anchor, storms actually cause the faithful ones to become even more anchored to their rock. The faithful ones look ahead. They understand that this world isn't their real home, and so they live for their heavenly home. This is what motivates and compels them to be faithful here. Something much better is coming, and they eagerly long for that day. Until then, they pursue an ever-growing faithful life.

The faithful know that life is full of tests. The faithful trust God and they pass these tests as they trust what God has said to them. Life is hard but God's promises can help us to endure triumphantly, knowing that His Word is true. This life isn't all there is, the best is yet to come, therefore, I can exalt Him through the pain, the loss, the tragedy. Even when the final test of death comes, the faithful trust God, which enables them to be at peace knowing that for the Christian, death is our best day. Death isn't the end, but the beginning of the glorious life with God. The faithful live with this belief, and they die with this belief.

The faithful ones fear God more than they fear men or what men can do to them. "They can hurt me and even kill me, but pain is fleeting, and death is gain." The faithful understand this. Therefore, the faithful stand up for God and His glory even when it brings pain. They honor God even when they stand alone. They even choose suffering over dishonoring God, for they look ahead in faith. Suffering for Christ is better than the easy life without Christ. God's glory is worth suffering and dying for. It's worth losing friends for. It's worth losing everything so long as He is pleased. The faithful understand this and they live it out more and more.

The faithful ones step out and obey God, even when stepping out looks ridiculous. They step out anyway. Their eyes are set on Him and they remain fixed. Even if it means getting thrown to the lions, and even if it means being tortured. The faithful ones know that God can rescue them at any time, but if He doesn't rescue them, they still won't compromise their faithfulness. They trust that if God wants to rescue them, then He will rescue them, but if He wants them to suffer and die, then they will suffer and die in faith for His glory. The faithful ones trust God in life and to the death. God is worth it, and so is the glory which lies ahead with Him.

No one has perfect faith, but we can certainly grow in it. The call is to learn from all these examples, to be challenged and encouraged in your faith, and to passionately pursue these things in your own walk of faith. So be encouraged and pursue. Examine yourself and see where your faith in action is lacking. Be encouraged by the faithfulness of others. Pursue these things in your life more and more until God takes you home. May these examples encourage you today. Be faithful to the end. By all means, be faithful to the end, He is certainly worth it.

APPENDIX
FAITH PRINCIPLES FROM HEBREWS 11

Faith Principle 1
The faithful trust in God as the Creator 12

Faith Principle 2
Abel: The faithful worship God from the heart 18

Faith Principle 3
Enoch: The faithful live to please God..33

Faith Principle 4
The faithful diligently seek God 36

Faith Principle 5
Noah: The faithful fear God 49

Faith Principle 6
The faithful obey God (Part I) 53

Faith Principle 7
Abraham: The faithful obey God (Part II) 60

Faith Principle 8
The faithful look ahead 65

Faith Principle 9
Sarah: The faithful embrace God's promises 72

Faith Principle 10
The Patriarchs: The faithful die trusting God 83

Faith Principle 11
The faithful embrace the promises of God 87

Faith Principle 12
The faithful live like strangers and pilgrims on the earth 89

Faith Principle 13
The faithful seek a homeland..................92

Faith Principle 14
The faithful desire a heavenly country 94

Faith Principle 15
Abraham: The faithful pass the test..................102

Faith Principle 16
Isaac: The faithful repent and bow to the providence of God..................121

Faith Principle 17
Jacob: The faithful take God at His Word 128

Faith Principle 18
Jacob: The faithful worship God 131

Faith Principle 19
Joseph: The faithful look ahead 132

Faith Principle 20
Moses' parents: The faithful don't fear..................140

Faith Principle 21
Moses: The faithful choose suffering over sin 148

Faith Principle 22
Moses: The faithful esteem reproaches over riches..................152

Faith Principle 23
Moses: The faithful look to the reward 153

Faith Principle 24
Moses: The faithful forsake the world for God's pleasure 158

Faith Principle 25
Moses: The faithful see Him who is invisible (Part II) 161

Faith Principle 26
Moses: The faithful obey (Part III) 162

Faith Principle 27
The children of Israel: The faithful step out..................................... 169

Faith Principle 28
The children of Israel: The faithful obey (Part IV) 174

Faith Principle 29
Rahab: The faithful stand alone.. 178

Faith Principle 30
Judges, prophets and others:
The faithful overcome and push ahead 185

Faith Principle 31
The prophets: The faithful put
God first, above men and even death... 192

Faith Principle 32
The faithful live for the next life... 196

Faith Principle 33
The faithful endure.. 211

Faith Principle 34
The faithful greatly please God... 214

BIBLIOGRAPHY

Allen, David. *Hebrews*, in The New American Commentary. Nashville, TN: B and H Publishing, 2010.

Applegarth, Margaret. *Junior Missionary Stories*. New York: Board of Publication and Bible School Work, 1917.

Barclay, William. "Hebrews." Study Light. https://www.studylight.org/commentaries/eng/dsb/hebrews-11.html. (Accessed on 4/3/2020).

Bauer, Walter. *A Greek-English Lexicon of the New Testament and Other Early Christian Literature*. Chicago: University of Chicago Press, 1979.

Bible.org. "The Mice family." Bible.org. https://bible.org/illustration/mice-family. (Accessed 4/14/2019).

Boice, James Montgomery. *Genesis: Vol. 1: An Expositional Commentary*. Grand Rapids: Baker Books, 1998.

Bonar, Andrew. *Memoir and Remains of Robert Murray M'Cheyne*. Edinburg: Banner of Truth Trust, 1995.

Bridges, Jerry. *The Joy of Fearing God*. Colorado Springs, CO: Waterbrook Press, 1998.

Bromily, G.W. *The International Standard Bible Encyclopedia*, vol. 2. Grand Rapids, MI: Eerdman's Publishing Co, 1982.

Brooks, Thomas. "Father Knows Best." Grace Gems. https://gracegems.org/Brooks/Mute%20Christian%20QUOTES.html (Accessed 3/23/2020).

Brown, Colin, ed. *The New International Dictionary of New Testament Theology*. 4 vols. Grand Rapids: Zondervan Publishing, 1986.

Brown, Francis, Samuel R. Driver, and Charles A. Briggs. *A Hebrew and English Lexicon of the Old Testament*. Oxford: Clarendon Press, 1975.

Brown, Raymond. *The Message of Hebrews*, in The Bible Speaks Today. Downers Grove, IL: Intervarsity Press, 1982.

Bunyan, John. *Pilgrims Progress in Modern English*. Chicago, IL: Moody Publishers, 1992.

Calhoun, David. *In Their Own Words*. Edinburgh: Banner of Truth Trust, 2018.

Carey, S. Pearce. *William Carey*. London: The Wakeman Trust, 1993.

Cole, Steven. "Upsetting the World for Christ." Acts: Lesson 43 (Acts 17:1-15). https://bible.org/seriespage/lesson-43-upsetting-world-christ-acts-171-15. (Accessed on 3/13, 2020).

Compelling Truth. "What Does it Mean That God is the Creator?" Got Questions Ministries, https://www.compellingtruth.org/Creator-God.html, (Accessed 7/21/2020).

Cowper, William. "God Moves in a Mysterious Way." Hymnal.net, https://www.hymnal.net/en/hymn/h/675 (Accessed 1/12/2022).

Ellingworth, Paul. *Hebrews*, in New International Greek Testament Commentary. Grand Rapids: Eerdmans Publishing Co., 1993.

Feinberg, Charles. *Jeremiah: A Commentary*. Grand Rapids: Zondervan, 1982.

Flanigan, J.M. *Hebrews*, in What the Bible Teaches. Avon: The Bath Press, 1997.

Foxe, John. *Foxe's Book of Martyrs*. Peabody, MA: Hendrickson Publishers, 2004.

Griffin, Edward. "Heaven." Grace Gems. https://gracegems.org/B/Griffin_heaven.html (Accessed on 1/25/2021).

Guzik, David. 'Genesis 22." Enduring Word. https://enduringword.com/bible-commentary/genesis-22.html (Accessed 5/23/2020).

Hendrickson, William, and Simon J. Kistemaker. *Exposition of Thessalonians, the Pastorals, and Hebrews*, in New Testament Commentary Series. Grand Rapids: Baker Academic, 2007.

Henry, Matthew. *Acts to Revelation*, in Matthew Henry's Commentary, vol. 4, reprint. McLean, Virginia: MacDonald Publishing, 1985.

Hewitt, Thomas. *The Epistle to the Hebrews*, in Tyndale New Testament Commentaries. Grand Rapids, MI: Eerdman's Publishing Co, 1981.

Hughes, Philip. *The Epistle to the Hebrews*, in New International Commentary of the New Testament. Grand Rapids, MI: Eerdman's Publishing Co, 1977.

Hughes, R. Kent, *Hebrews*, in Preaching the Word. Wheaton, IL: Crossway, 2015.

Johnson, S. Lewis. "The Faith of the Patriarchs: Hebrews." SLJ Institute. https://sljinstitute.net/general-epistles/hebrews/the-faith-of-the-patriarchs-hebrews/html (accessed 6/22/2020).

Kittel, Gerhard, and Gerhard Freidrich. *The Theological Dictionary of the New Testament*. Trans. By Geoffrey Bromily. 10 vols. Grand Rapids: Eerdmans Publishing, 1984.

Lechler, G.V. ed. Phillip Schaff. "Hus, John." *A Religious Encyclopedia or Dictionary of Biblical, Historical, Doctrinal, and Practical Theology*. Toronto. New York & London: Funk & Wagnalls, 1894.

Liddell, H. *A lexicon: Abridged from Liddell and Scott's Greek-English lexicon*. 2 vols. Oak Harbor, WA: Logos Research Systems, Inc., 1996.

Louw, Johannes P. and Eugene A. Nida, eds. *Greek-English Lexicon of the New Testament*. New York: United Bible Society, 1988.

Maclaren, Alexander. *Expositions of Holy Scripture: 2Corinthians*. Grand Rapids: Eerdman's Publishing, 1944.

Marshall, Alfred. *The New International Version Interlinear Greek-English New Testament*. Grand Rapids: Zondervan Publishing, 1976.

MacArthur, John. *2 Corinthians*, in The MacArthur New Testament Commentary. Chicago: Moody Bible Institute, 2003.

_____. *Matthew*, in The MacArthur Commentary Series. Chicago, IL: Moody Press, 1988.

Mccomiskey, T.E., eds R. L. Harris, G. L. Archer Jr., & B. K. Waltke. *Theological Wordbook of the Old Testament*. Chicago: Moody Press, 1981.

McMahon, Matthew. "The Reformation." A Puritan's Mind. http://www.apuritansmind.com/Reformation/Reformation.htm (Accessed 8/14/08).

Moody, D.L. *Moody's Anecdotes.* Chicago: Moody Press, 1898.

Moore, Thomas. Good Reads, https://www.goodreads.com/quotes/774409-fight-on-my-men-says-sir-andrew-barton-i-am-hurt-but (accessed 1/12/2022).

Morris, Henry. *The Genesis Record.* Grand Rapids, MI: Baker Book house, 181.

Owen, John. *An Exposition of Hebrews*, vol. 4, in Puritan Classics. Marshalltown, DE: The national Foundation for Christian Education, 1969.

Phillips, Richard. *Hebrews*, in Reformed Expository Commentary. Phillipsburg, New Jersey: P&R Publishing, 2006.

Pink, A. W. *An Exposition of Hebrews.* Grand Rapids, MI: Baker Book House, 1954.

Piper, John. "The Unashamed God." Desiring God. https://www.desiringgod.org/articles /the-unashamed-god. (Accessed 8/22/2020).

_____ "Faith Makes the Difference When We Walk Through Crisis." Desiring God. https://www.desiringgod.org/messages/liberated-for-love-by-looking-to-the-reward (Accessed 4/14/2020).

_____ "Immortal Till His Work Was Done: John Paton (1824–1907)." Desiring God. https://www.desiringgod.org/articles/immortal-till-his-work-was-done (Accessed 4/22/2020).

_____ "Faith to Be Strong and Faith to Be Weak." Desiring God. https://www.desiring god.org/messages/faith-to-be-strong-and-faith-to-be-weak (Accessed 1/12/2022).

Precept Austin. "Hebrews." Precept Austin. https://www.preceptaustin.org/hebrews_11_sermon_illustrations (Accessed 5/3/2020).

Ryle, J.C. *Holiness*. Moscow, ID: Charles Nolan Publishers, 2002.

Spurgeon, Charles. "Spurgeon's verse expositions of the Bible: Genesis." Study Light. https://www.studylight.org/commentaries/eng/spe/genesis-22.html (accessed 3/25/2020).

_____ "Watch-Night Service." Bible Bulletin Board. https://www.biblebb.com/files/spurgeon/0059.HTM (Accessed 1/12/2022).

_____ "The Two Pivots." Spurgeon Gems. https://www.spurgeongems.org/sermon/chs2633.pdf (Accessed 4/5/2020).

_____ *The Treasury of David*, vol. 1. Peabody, MA: Hendrickson Publishers.

Studd, C.T. "Only One Life, Twill Soon Be Past – by C.T. Studd." Reasons for Hope. https://reasonsforhopejesus.com/only-one-life-twill-soon-be-past-by-c-t-studd-1860-1931/ (Accessed 1/25/2022).

Sumner, Robert L. *Hebrews Streams of Living Water*. Raleigh, NC: Biblical Evangelism, 2003.

Tozer, A.W. "Man: The Dwelling Place of God." https://www.worldinvisible.com/library/tozer/5j00.0010/5j00.0010.07.htm. (Accessed 2/3/2020).

Vincent, Marvin. *Word Studies in the New Testament*, vol. 4. Grand Rapids: Eerdman's Publishing Co: 1957.

Vine, W.E. *Vines Expository Dictionary of Old and New Testament Words*. Old Tappan, New Jersey: Fleming H. Revell Co., 1981.

Watson, Thomas. "The Lord's Prayer." Grace Gems. https://www.gracegems. org/Watson /lords_prayer4.htm (Accessed 5/4/2020).

Wenk, Elizabeth, *John Muir Trail*. Birmingham: Wilderness press, 2014.

Wilson, Geoffrey. *Hebrews*. Edinburgh: The Banner of Truth Trust, 1979.

Wuest, Kenneth. *Wuest's Word Studies from the Greek New Testament: for the English reader*, vol. 10. Grand Rapids, MI: Eerdmans, 1997.

Wylie, James. "John Huss and the Hussite Wars." Doctrine. http://www.doctrine.org/history /HPv1b3.htm#CHAPTER%207 (Accessed 8/17/09).

Zaimov, Stoyan. "21 Coptic Christians Beheaded by ISIS Honored for Refusing to Deny Christ." Christian Post. https://www.christianpost.com/news/21-coptic-christians-beheaded-by-isis-honored-refusing-deny-christ.html (accessed 1/12/2022).

www.ingramcontent.com/pod-product-compliance
Lightning Source LLC
Chambersburg PA
CBHW060519080526
44586CB00012B/540